A VISUAL GUIDE TO
BIRDS

Rosen
YA
New York

SOL90 EDITORIAL STAFF

This edition published in 2019 by:
The Rosen Publishing Group, Inc.
29 East 21st Street
New York, NY 10010

Cataloging-in-Publication Data

Names: Editorial Sol 90 (Firm).
Title: A visual guide to birds / edited by the Sol 90 Editorial Staff.
Description: New York : Rosen YA, 2019. | Series: A visual exploration of science | Includes glossary and index.
Identifiers: LCCN ISBN 9781508182320 (pbk.) | ISBN 9781508182313 (library bound)
Subjects: LCSH: Birds—Juvenile literature. | Birds—Identification—Juvenile literature.
Classification: LCC QL676.2 V578 2019 | DDC 598—dc23

Manufactured in the United States of America

Project Management: Nuria Cicero
Editorial Coordination: Alberto Hernández, Joan Soriano, Diana Malizia
Proofreaders: Marta Kordon, Edgardo D'Elio
Layout: Laura Ocampo

Photo Credits: Age Fotostock, Getty Images, Science Photo Library, Graphic News, ESA, NASA, National Geographic, Latinstock, Album, ACI, Cordon Press, Shutterstock

Illustrators: Guido Arroyo, Pablo Aschei, Gustavo J. Caironi, Hernán Cañellas, Leonardo César, José Luis Corsetti, Vanina Farías, Manrique Fernández Buente, Joana Garrido, Celina Hilbert, Jorge Ivanovich, Isidro López, Diego Martín, Jorge Martínez, Marco Menco, Marcelo Morán, Ala de Mosca, Diego Mourelos, Eduardo Pérez, Javier Pérez, Ariel Piroyansky, Fernando Ramallo, Ariel Roldán, Marcel Socías, Néstor Taylor, Trebol Animation, Juan Venegas, Constanza Vicco, Coralia Vignau, Gustavo Yamin, 3DN, 3DOM studio.

Contents

A Universe of Birds

Welcome to the world of birds. No matter how you approach it, this is a wonderful book not only for its pictures, splendid illustrations, size, and format but also because, as you read it, you will discover secrets about these inhabitants of the Earth, which, according to the history of evolution, came into being before humans. The text is written in a direct, easy-to-understand style. Most birds have a much-envied ability that has inspired poems and all types of experiments: they can fly. This enables them to see expansive terrains from afar, full of seas, mountains, rivers, cities, and other features. It has been estimated that more than 200 million birds migrate all over the planet each year. Many of them

fly thousands of miles, crossing desolate deserts and windy seas to arrive in Africa or Antarctica. Some find their way using the sun, the moon, and the stars; others follow their parents or use the course of rivers or mountain chains as references. In general, smaller birds migrating across continents stop several times to get food. It is surprising how fast they travel, in spite of these stops: it has been calculated that some small species cover almost 2,500 miles (4,000 km) in five or six days. Several studies have shown that carrier pigeons and white-headed sparrows, for example, can travel more than 600 miles (1,000 km) per day. Some ducks, such as the blue-winged teal, complete their trip from Canada to central Mexico in about 35 days, making several stops to feed along the way.

Birds never cease to amaze us, whether hiding in trees, flying over high mountaintops, or nesting in Antarctica or on tall buildings. Perhaps the reason for such amazement is their behavior, which continues to be a mystery to human beings, as well as the differences among them. It is believed that there are approximately 9,700 living species of birds in the world—more than in any other vertebrate group except for fish. Once they reach adulthood, birds' weight varies from a mere 0.06 ounces (1.6 g), in the case of hummingbirds, to as much as 330 pounds (150 kg) for African ostriches. While most birds fly, there are some—such as kiwis, rheas, and ostriches—that run quickly on the ground. Some birds, being perfectly adapted to aquatic life, live in oceans, rivers, and lakes. The shape of their feet and bills varies according to the environment in which they live. Some aquatic species have bills modified to filter small water particles, whereas birds of prey have strong bills that are bent, allowing them to hold down and tear apart their prey. What is the diet of birds based on? Because of their great diversity and wide distribution, their diets differ greatly. In general, birds eat a bit of everything, although insects are the most important element of their diet. They eat fruit, seeds, nectar, pollen, leaves, carrion, and other vertebrates. Most birds lay their eggs in nests. Both males and females are particularly protective toward their young. Adult birds care for their chicks, warn and protect them against the danger of predators, and guide them to safe places where they can live and feed. We invite you to investigate up close the world of these fascinating beings that are able to run, climb, swim, dive, and cross the skies. ●

The Nature of Birds

Many scientists maintain that birds descended from dinosaurs because fossils of dinosaur specimens with feathers have been found.

As a group, birds have exceptional eyesight—they have the largest eyes in relation to the size of their bodies. In addition, they have very light bones, which are suitable for flight. Just like

OWL *(Bubo capensis)*
This owl is native to Africa. It feeds on birds and mammals.

their bills, birds' feet have also changed in accordance with the functions and particular needs of each species. For instance, walking birds—like other vertebrate groups—display a marked tendency toward having a reduced number of toes; ostriches, for example, have only two. Some birds of prey, such as eagles, have feet that are veritable hooks. ●

Beyond Feathers

D efining what a bird is brings to mind an animal covered with feathers that has a toothless bill and anterior extremities morphed into wings. Other distinguishing characteristics are that they are warm-blooded and have pneumatic bones—bones filled with air chambers instead of marrow. Birds have very efficient circulatory and respiratory systems and great neuromuscular and sensory coordination. ●

Variety and Uniformity

We can find birds in every type of environment: aquatic, aerial, and terrestrial, in polar regions and in tropical zones. Their adaptation to the environment has been very successful. Nevertheless, birds are one of the groups that display the fewest differences among their members.

WINE-THROATED HUMMINGBIRD

0.06 ounces (1.6 g)

WEIGHT OF THE SMALLEST BIRD

AFRICAN OSTRICH

330 pounds (150 kg)

WEIGHT OF THE LARGEST BIRD

PENGUIN

-75 F (-60° C)

THE TEMPERATURE PENGUINS ENDURE IN ANTARCTICA

WHITE-THROATED SPARROW
A small bird that lives in North America and on the Iberian Peninsula

Adaptation to Flying

Some crucial anatomic and physiological characteristics explain birds' ability to fly. Their bodies and feathers reduce friction with the air and improve lift. Their strong muscles, light bones, air sacs, and closed double circulatory system also play a role in their ability to fly.

FEATHERS
Feathers are a unique characteristic of birds. No other living animal has them. They are appealing for their structure, variety, and constant renewal.

WINGS
Wings propel, maintain, and guide birds during flight. They have modified bones and characteristic plumage.

105.8°F (41° C) **IS THEIR BODY TEMPERATURE.**

COVERTS

FLIGHT FEATHERS

UNDERTAIL COVERTS

THIGH

STRUCTURE
Birds find their balance in movement. A bird's internal architecture contributes to its stability. The location of its feet and wings helps to concentrate its weight close to its center of gravity.

TAIL
The last vertebrae merges into the pygostyle. The tail feathers develop in this area.

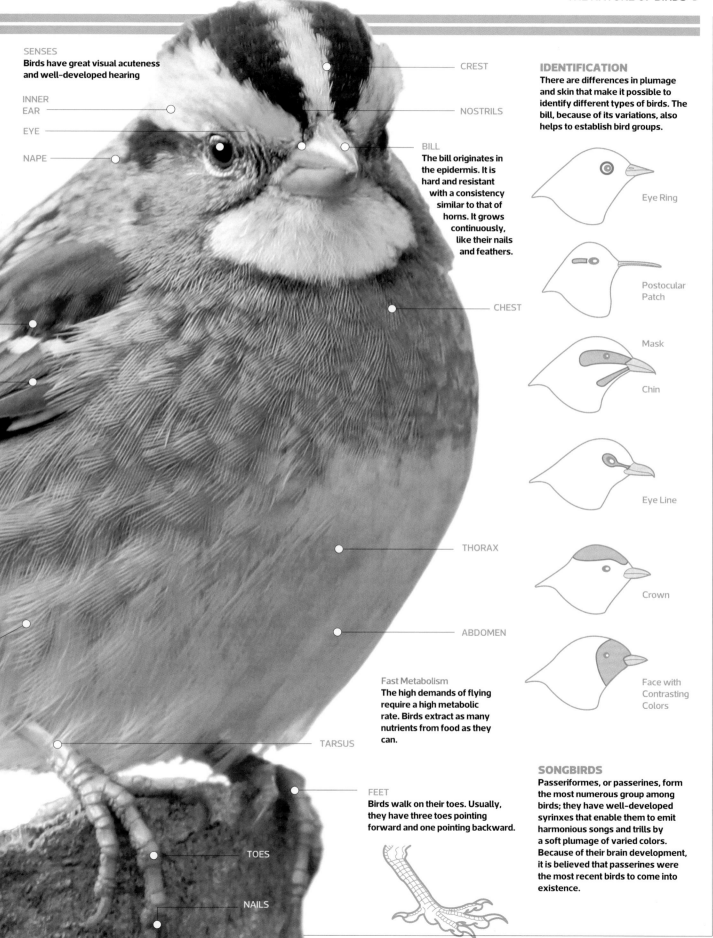

SENSES
Birds have great visual acuteness and well-developed hearing

INNER EAR

EYE

NAPE

CREST

NOSTRILS

BILL
The bill originates in the epidermis. It is hard and resistant with a consistency similar to that of horns. It grows continuously, like their nails and feathers.

CHEST

THORAX

ABDOMEN

Fast Metabolism
The high demands of flying require a high metabolic rate. Birds extract as many nutrients from food as they can.

TARSUS

FEET
Birds walk on their toes. Usually, they have three toes pointing forward and one pointing backward.

TOES

NAILS

IDENTIFICATION

There are differences in plumage and skin that make it possible to identify different types of birds. The bill, because of its variations, also helps to establish bird groups.

Eye Ring

Postocular Patch

Mask

Chin

Eye Line

Crown

Face with Contrasting Colors

SONGBIRDS

Passeriformes, or passerines, form the most numerous group among birds; they have well-developed syrinxes that enable them to emit harmonious songs and trills by a soft plumage of varied colors. Because of their brain development, it is believed that passerines were the most recent birds to come into existence.

Origin

The evolution of birds is a hot topic that is still being debated by scientists today. The most widespread theory states that birds descended from theropods, dinosaurs that walked on two legs. Fossils of dinosaur specimens with feathers have been found, and Archaeopteryx, a primitive bird that lived 150 million years ago, is the oldest relative known. Completely covered with feathers, it had a pair of wings that enabled it to fly. However, it retained many dinosaur traits. ●

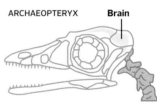

Archaeopteryx lithographica

The oldest relative lived in the Jurassic Period, 150 million years ago.

Comparison to a human

Order	Saurischians
Suborder	Theropods
Diet	Carnivore
Length	10 inches (25 cm)
Height	8 to 12 inches (20-30 cm)
Weight	18 ounces (500 g)

REPTILIAN JAWBONES WITH TEETH
Unlike modern birds, it did not have a horn bill. Instead, the Archaeopteryx had a tight row of sharp teeth on each jawbone.

SPINE
It had a movable spine. The cervical vertebrae have a concave joint like that of the theropods, not a saddle-shaped one like that of birds.

From Reptile to Bird

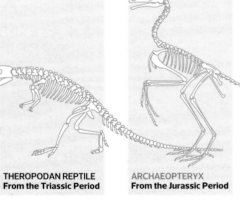

THEROPODAN REPTILE
From the Triassic Period

ARCHAEOPTERYX
From the Jurassic Period

PIGEON **Alive**
Today

SKULL
Surprisingly, its skull is similar to that of present-day reptiles and early theropods. The arrangement of the brain and ears reveals that it had a great sense of orientation and that it was able to perform complicated maneuvers.

ARCHAEOPTERYX   **Brain**

MODERN BIRD

Fossils

Several fossil samples were found between 1861 and 1993. The first one, found in Bavaria, Germany, was very important because its discovery coincided with the publication of *On the Origin of Species* by Charles Darwin, at a time when the search for evolutionary "missing links" fascinated scientists. The original is located in the British Museum. Another fossil, which includes the head, is in the Berlin Museum.

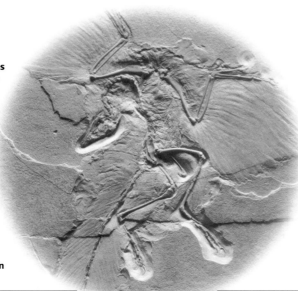

FROM ARMS TO WINGS
It had a greater range of motion in the upper limbs than primitive dinosaurs.

ARCHAEOPTERYX
150 million years ago

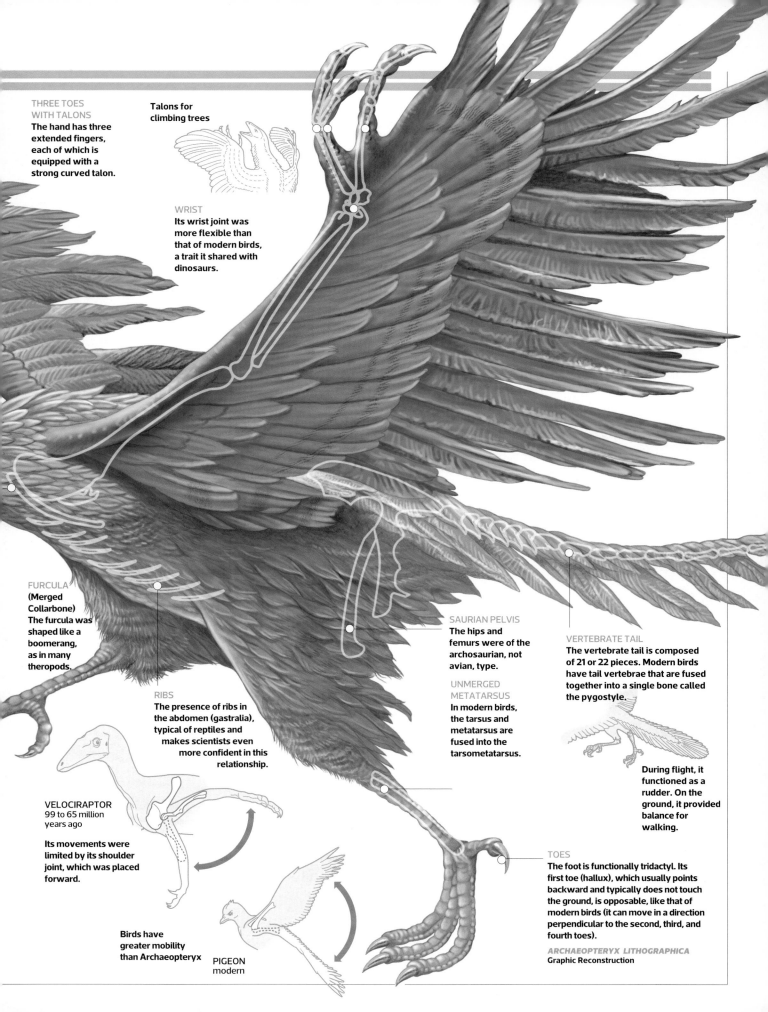

THREE TOES WITH TALONS
The hand has three extended fingers, each of which is equipped with a strong curved talon.

Talons for climbing trees

WRIST
Its wrist joint was more flexible than that of modern birds, a trait it shared with dinosaurs.

FURCULA
(Merged Collarbone)
The furcula was shaped like a boomerang, as in many theropods.

RIBS
The presence of ribs in the abdomen (gastralia), typical of reptiles and makes scientists even more confident in this relationship.

SAURIAN PELVIS
The hips and femurs were of the archosaurian, not avian, type.

UNMERGED METATARSUS
In modern birds, the tarsus and metatarsus are fused into the tarsometatarsus.

VERTEBRATE TAIL
The vertebrate tail is composed of 21 or 22 pieces. Modern birds have tail vertebrae that are fused together into a single bone called the pygostyle.

During flight, it functioned as a rudder. On the ground, it provided balance for walking.

VELOCIRAPTOR
99 to 65 million years ago

Its movements were limited by its shoulder joint, which was placed forward.

Birds have greater mobility than Archaeopteryx

PIGEON
modern

TOES
The foot is functionally tridactyl. Its first toe (hallux), which usually points backward and typically does not touch the ground, is opposable, like that of modern birds (it can move in a direction perpendicular to the second, third, and fourth toes).

ARCHAEOPTERYX LITHOGRAPHICA
Graphic Reconstruction

Skeleton and Musculature

B oth lightweight and resistant, the skeleton of birds underwent important changes in order to adapt to flight. Some bones, like those of the skull and wings, fused to become lighter. Birds have fewer bones than other vertebrates. Because their bones are hollow, containing internal air chambers, the total weight of their bones is less than that of their feathers. Birds' spines tend to be very flexible in the cervical region but rigid near the rib cage, where a large, curved frontal bone, the sternum, attaches. The sternum features a large keel to which the pectoral muscles attach. These large, strong muscles are used for flapping the wings. In contrast, running birds, such as ostriches, have more developed muscles in their legs. ●

EYE SOCKET

Flapping Wings

Flying demands an enormous amount of energy and strength. Consequently, the muscles responsible for flapping the wings become very large, easily comprising 15 percent of the weight of a flying bird. Two pairs of pectorals, in which one muscle of the pair is bigger than the other, work to raise and lower the wings. They function symmetrically and in opposition to each other: when one contracts, the other relaxes. Their placement within the thoracic cavity corresponds roughly to the bird's center of gravity. The motion of the wings also requires strong tendons.

HUMMINGBIRD
Because of its adaptation to stationary flight, a hummingbird's pectoral muscles can account for 40 percent of its total weight.

SKULL
Light because of the fusing of bones, the skull does not have teeth, a bony jaw, or grinding muscles.

UPPER MANDIBLE OF BILL
In some species, it is flexible.

LOWER MANDIBLE OF BILL
It is flexible, allowing birds to open their mouths wide.

FURCULA (COLLARBONE)
Known as the wishbone, it is unique to birds and results from the fusion of the collarbones.

STERNUM
Hyperdeveloped in flying birds, the sternum's long keel facilitates the attachment of the pectorals.

WINGS

Without a doubt, wings are the greatest adaptation of birds. Strong tendons travel through the wings and merge into the hand bones, where the feathers are attached.

DOWNWARD FLAP

1.
The **larger pectorals** contract.

Right Wing
Humerus
Coracoids
Tendon
Left Wing
Keel
Legs

2.
The descending flapping of the wings takes place.

The **smaller pectorals** relax.

UPWARD FLAP

1.
The **pectoral muscles** relax.

Tendon
Right Wing
Humerus
Coracoids
Left Wing
Legs

2.
The **smaller pectorals** contract and draw the wings inward.

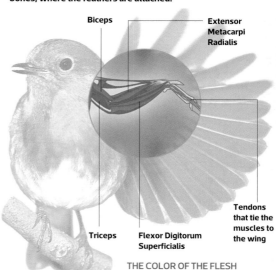

Biceps
Extensor Metacarpi Radialis
Triceps
Flexor Digitorum Superficialis
Tendons that tie the muscles to the wing

THE COLOR OF THE FLESH
depends on the blood circulation in the muscles: the more circulation, the redder the flesh. Flying birds have red flesh, whereas nonflying birds, such as chickens, have white flesh.

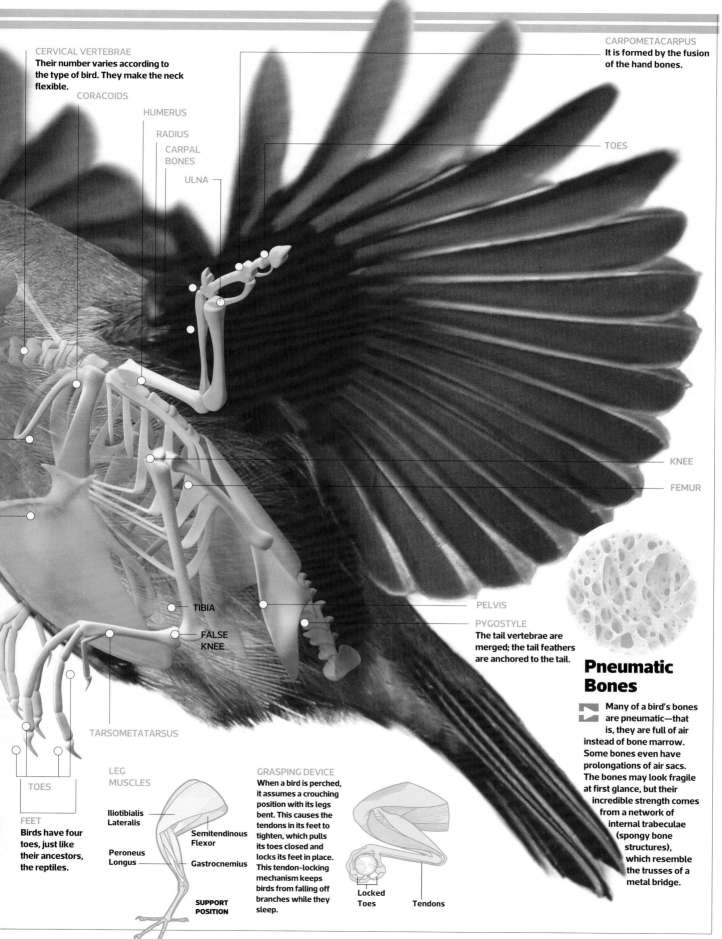

CERVICAL VERTEBRAE
Their number varies according to the type of bird. They make the neck flexible.

CORACOIDS

HUMERUS

RADIUS

CARPAL BONES

ULNA

CARPOMETACARPUS
It is formed by the fusion of the hand bones.

TOES

KNEE

FEMUR

TIBIA

FALSE KNEE

TARSOMETATARSUS

PELVIS

PYGOSTYLE
The tail vertebrae are merged; the tail feathers are anchored to the tail.

TOES

FEET
Birds have four toes, just like their ancestors, the reptiles.

LEG MUSCLES

Iliotibialis Lateralis

Semitendinous Flexor

Peroneus Longus

Gastrocnemius

SUPPORT POSITION

GRASPING DEVICE
When a bird is perched, it assumes a crouching position with its legs bent. This causes the tendons in its feet to tighten, which pulls its toes closed and locks its feet in place. This tendon-locking mechanism keeps birds from falling off branches while they sleep.

Locked Toes

Tendons

Pneumatic Bones

Many of a bird's bones are pneumatic—that is, they are full of air instead of bone marrow. Some bones even have prolongations of air sacs. The bones may look fragile at first glance, but their incredible strength comes from a network of internal trabeculae (spongy bone structures), which resemble the trusses of a metal bridge.

Internal Organs

Birds in flight can consume oxygen at a rate that a well-trained athlete would not be able to withstand for even a few minutes. Because of this oxygen consumption, all their organs have had to adapt. The lungs of birds, though smaller than those of mammals of similar size, are much more efficient. Their lungs have several air sacs that both increase the efficiency of their respiratory systems and make them lighter. A special feature of the digestive system is a crop in the esophagus, where food is stored for digestion or for feeding the young. A bird's heart can be four times larger in relation to its body size than a human's in relation to its body size. ●

Digestive System

Birds have no teeth. Therefore, they ingest food without chewing, and their stomachs break it down. The stomach is divided into two parts: the glandular (or proventriculus) part, which secretes acids, and the muscular (or gizzard) part, whose muscular walls grind up what is eaten. In general, the process is very fast because flying requires a lot of energy, and the bird has to replenish that energy quickly. The digestive system ends at the cloaca, which is an excretory orifice shared with the urinary system. Birds absorb almost all the water they drink.

FOOD ITINERARY

1 STORAGE
Some birds have a crop, which enables them to store food and digest it later. This also allows them to decrease their exposure to predators.

2 PRODUCTION
The proventriculus secretes the gastric juices that initiate digestion.

3 BREAKDOWN
In the gizzard, a strong and muscular pouch, food is broken down with the help of swallowed stones or sand. The stones and sand play the role of teeth.

4 WATER ABSORPTION
Water is absorbed in the small intestine. Birds normally get water from the food they ingest.

5 EXCRETION
The cloaca expels feces mixed with urine coming from the excretory system.

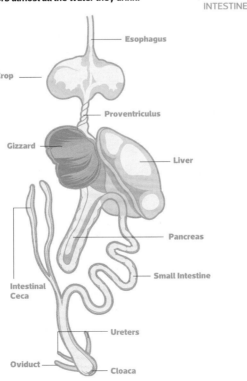

Esophagus
Crop
Proventriculus
Gizzard
Liver
Pancreas
Small Intestine
Intestinal Ceca
Ureters
Oviduct
Cloaca

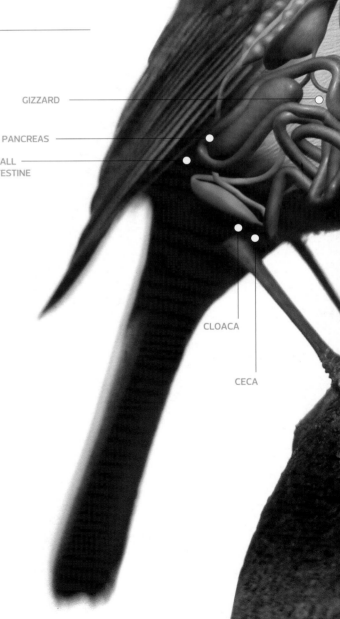

GIZZARD
PANCREAS
SMALL INTESTINE
CLOACA
CECA

TYPES OF GIZZARD

Granivorous Birds have thick muscle walls and strong mucous membranes (or internal skin) to break down seeds.

Carnivorous Birds have thin muscle walls because digestion takes place in the proventriculus.

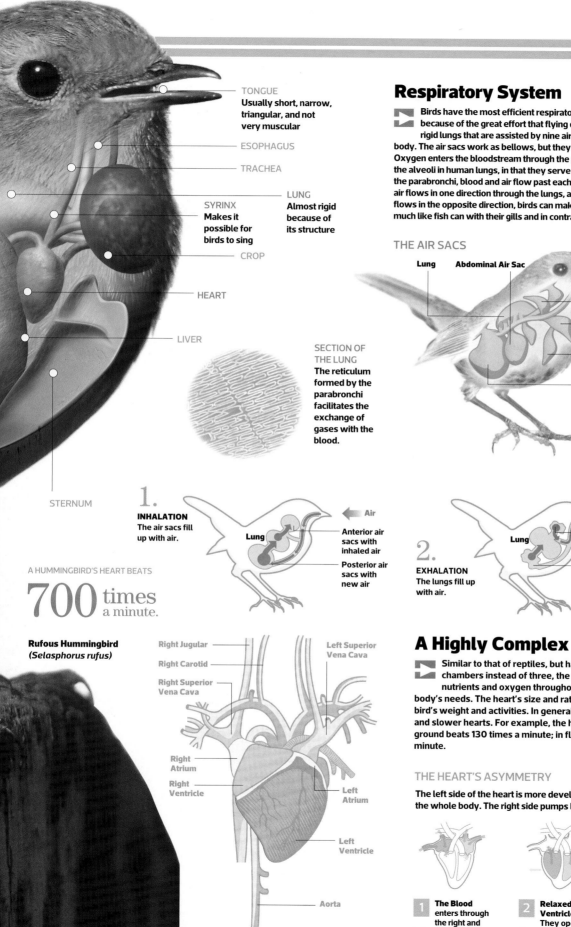

TONGUE
Usually short, narrow, triangular, and not very muscular

ESOPHAGUS

TRACHEA

SYRINX
Makes it possible for birds to sing

LUNG
Almost rigid because of its structure

CROP

HEART

LIVER

STERNUM

SECTION OF THE LUNG
The reticulum formed by the parabronchi facilitates the exchange of gases with the blood.

A HUMMINGBIRD'S HEART BEATS

700 times a minute.

Rufous Hummingbird
(*Selasphorus rufus*)

Respiratory System

Birds have the most efficient respiratory system of any vertebrate because of the great effort that flying demands. It has two small, almost rigid lungs that are assisted by nine air sacs distributed throughout the body. The air sacs work as bellows, but they do not carry out gas exchange. Oxygen enters the bloodstream through the parabronchi, which are much like the alveoli in human lungs, in that they serve as the tissue for gas exchange. In the parabronchi, blood and air flow past each other in tiny passages. Because air flows in one direction through the lungs, and blood in the lung capillaries flows in the opposite direction, birds can make use of all the air they inhale, much like fish can with their gills and in contrast with mammals, which cannot.

THE AIR SACS

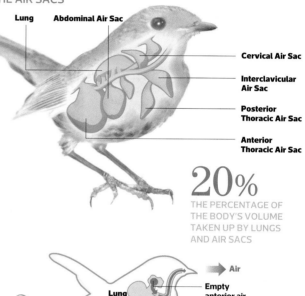

Lung   **Abdominal Air Sac**

Cervical Air Sac

Interclavicular Air Sac

Posterior Thoracic Air Sac

Anterior Thoracic Air Sac

20%
THE PERCENTAGE OF THE BODY'S VOLUME TAKEN UP BY LUNGS AND AIR SACS

1.
INHALATION
The air sacs fill up with air.

Lung

Air

Anterior air sacs with inhaled air

Posterior air sacs with new air

2.
EXHALATION
The lungs fill up with air.

Lung

Air

Empty anterior air sacs

Empty posterior air sacs

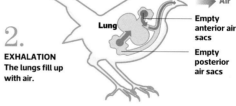

Right Jugular

Right Carotid

Right Superior Vena Cava

Right Atrium

Right Ventricle

Left Superior Vena Cava

Left Atrium

Left Ventricle

Aorta

A Highly Complex Heart

Similar to that of reptiles, but having a heart with four chambers instead of three, the circulatory system distributes nutrients and oxygen throughout the body according to the body's needs. The heart's size and rate vary depending on the bird's weight and activities. In general, bigger birds have smaller and slower hearts. For example, the heart of a seagull on the ground beats 130 times a minute; in flight, it beats 625 times a minute.

THE HEART'S ASYMMETRY

The left side of the heart is more developed, because it pumps blood to the whole body. The right side pumps blood only to the lungs.

1 **The Blood**
enters through the right and left arteries.

2 **Relaxed Ventricles**
They open the atrioventricular valves.

3 **Contracted Ventricles**
The blood enters the bloodstream.

The Senses

n birds, the sense organs are concentrated on the head, except for the sense of touch, which is found all over the body. Birds have the largest eyes with respect to the size of their bodies. This enables them to see distant objects with considerable precision. Their field of vision is very broad, over 300 degrees, but in general they have little binocular vision. The ear—a simple orifice, but very refined in nocturnal hunters—helps them notice sounds inaudible to humans, which facilitates the detection of prey while flying. The senses of touch and smell, on the other hand, are important only to some birds, and the sense of taste is almost nonexistent. ●

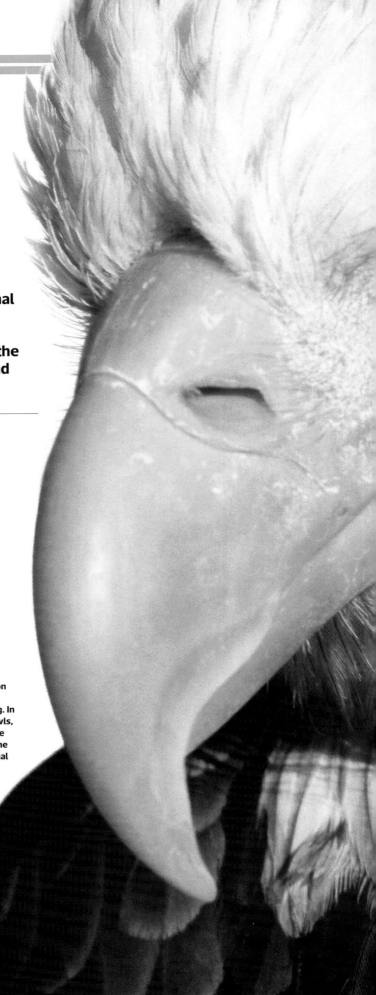

The Ear

Birds' ears are simpler than those of mammals: a bird's ear has no outer portion, and in some cases, it is covered with rigid feathers. A notable part of the ear is the columella—a bone that birds share with reptiles. The ear is nonetheless well developed, and birds have very acute hearing; whereas human beings can detect just one note, birds can detect many. The ear is essential to a bird's balance, a key factor in flying. It is also believed that in certain species the ear works as a barometer, indicating altitude.

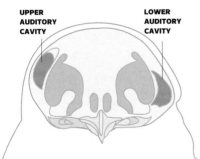

UPPER AUDITORY CAVITY

LOWER AUDITORY CAVITY

LOCATION OF THE EARS

Located at different heights on the head, the ears cause the slight delay in a bird's hearing. In nocturnal hunters, such as owls, this asymmetry allows for the triangulation of sounds and the tracking of prey with a minimal margin of error.

Touch, Taste, and Smell

The sense of touch is well developed in the bill and tongue of many birds, especially in those birds that use them to find food, such as shore birds and woodpeckers. Usually the tongue is narrow, with few taste buds, but sufficient enough to distinguish among salty, sweet, bitter, and acidic tastes. The sense of smell is not very developed: although the cavity is broad, the olfactory epithelium is reduced. In some birds, such as kiwis and scavengers (condors, for example), the olfactory epithelium is more developed.

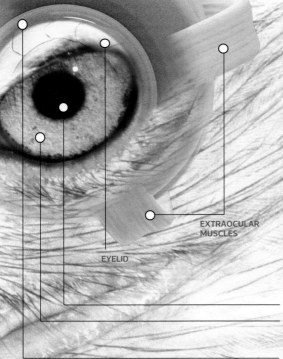

Vision

is the most developed sense in birds because some flight maneuvers, as well as the recognition of food from afar, depend on it. Birds have relatively large eyes. In most cases, they are wider than they are deep because the lens and the cornea—which is supported by a series of sclerotic bony plates—project beyond the eye socket. In hunting birds, the eyes are almost tubular. The muscles around the eye change their shape, alter the lens, and create greater visual acuity: birds typically have a 20-fold magnification (and sometimes, as in the case of some diving birds, a 60-fold magnification), in comparison with humans. Their sensitivity to light is also remarkable, with some species being able to recognize light spectra invisible to the human eye.

EXTRAOCULAR MUSCLES

EYELID

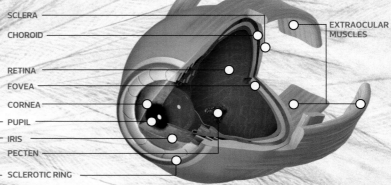

SCLERA
CHOROID
RETINA
FOVEA
CORNEA
PUPIL
IRIS
PECTEN
SCLEROTIC RING

EXTRAOCULAR MUSCLES

FIELD OF VISION

The eyes—when located on the sides of the head, as is the case with most birds—create a broad field of vision: more than 300 degrees. Each eye covers different areas, focusing on the same object only when looking ahead through a narrow binocular field of vision.

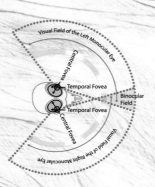

Visual Field of the Left Monocular Eye
Central Fovea
Temporal Fovea
Binocular Field
Temporal Fovea
Central Fovea
Visual Field of the Right Monocular Eye

THE HUMAN FIELD OF VISION

The eyes, located at the front, move together, covering the same area. Because human beings cannot move their eyes independently from each other, they have only binocular vision.

Visual Field of the Left Monocular Eye
Binocular Field
Visual Field of the Right Monocular Eye

COMPARISON OF BINOCULAR FIELDS OF VISION

Binocular vision is essential for measuring distances without making mistakes. The brain processes the images that each eye generates separately as if they were a single image. The small differences between the two images allow the brain to create a third one in depth, or in three dimensions. Hunting birds, for which the correct perception of distance is a life-and-death matter, tend to have eyes located toward the front, with a wide field of binocular vision. In contrast, birds with lateral eyes calculate distance by moving their heads, but they record a larger total field of vision to avoid becoming prey. Owls are the birds with the greatest binocular vision—up to 70 degrees.

HUNTING BIRDS' FIELD OF VISION

Frontal eyes reduce the total field of vision but allow for a wide field of binocular vision.

A
B

BINOCULAR FIELD OF VISION
MONOCULAR FIELD OF VISION

NONHUNTING BIRDS' FIELD OF VISION

The lateral eyes open the field of vision to as much as 360 degrees but reduce the binocular field.

A
B

MONOCULAR FIELD OF VISION
BINOCULAR FIELD OF VISION

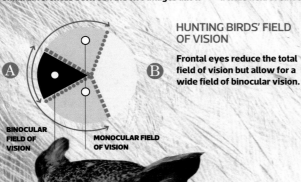

A
B

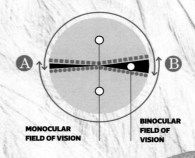

A
B

Different Types of Bills

The beak, or bill, is a projecting structure of horn—made out of the same material as the nails—that grows as it is worn down. In the case of adult birds, bill size remains constant. The bill is joined to the skull in a way that allows for the movement of the lower mandible and, thus, the opening of the mouth. Most birds depend on their bills to get food. There are many types of bills, that differ in size, shape, color, and hardness, depending on the way in which the bird gets its food.

UPPER JAW

LOWER JAW

CHIN

NOSTRIL

COMMISSURE

GONYS

You Are What You Eat

There is a close relationship between a bird's bill and its diet. Because the bill serves to pick up, hunt, tear, and transport the food, depending on the bird's lifestyle, its appearance is related to the bird's diet. If the diet is very specific, the bill tends to have an adapted, unique shape, as is the case with hummingbirds. Omnivorous birds, on the other hand, have simple bills with no special alterations that are suitable for all tasks.

PREMAXILLA

UPPER MAXILLARY BONE

LOWER MAXILLARY BONE

DENTARY

COMPOSITION AND STRUCTURE

The jaws are covered with a hard horn layer called the ramphotheca, which is the external, visible portion. This determines the bill's color.

Parts of the Bill

Each jaw has characteristic elements. In the upper one, from the back to the front, are the nostrils (or nasal cavities), the culmen (or maxillary cover), and the tip, which, in carnivorous birds, contains the tomial, or killing, tooth. In the lower jaw is the gonys, or cover. The variations found in each part of the bill are conditioned by the bill's function.

CULMEN

Hardness

Its long, stout bill is extraordinarily hard. Despite its appearance, the bill is very light, and birds can use it adeptly to seize and to open the fruits they eat.

TIP

Heterogeneous Shapes

Bills have a wide array of names and shapes, but they are usually classified according to their length in relation to the head (short or long); to the curvature of its axis (pointing upward or downward); to its width; to its general shape (conical, stiletto-shaped, or spatula-shaped); and to the presence or absence of accessory pieces, such as grooves, horny plates, or false serrated teeth.

TOUCANS AND ARICARI

With their long, thick bills, they can reach fruit located on branches that are too thin for the bird to sit on. Their bills are also used to break the peels and seeds of fruits.

FLAMINGO

Flamingos have thin, threadlike structures inside their bills whose function is similar to that of the baleen of whales. They feed on microorganisms through filtration.

HERON

The heron fishes in shallow waters and has a long, solid, sharp bill that quickly slices through the water to easily harpoon fish.

GREENFINCH

Like granivores in general, it has a strong, conical bill, used to detach seeds from plants and, sometimes, to crack them.

FALCON

It uses the false (tomial) tooth at the tip to detach the flesh from the bone and to break the spine of its prey.

RAVEN

Because of its unrestricted diet, its bill is simple and relatively long.

HUMMINGBIRD

The ability to reach the bottom of a flower in order to suck nectar requires not only a long, thin bill but also a special tongue.

CROSSBILL

It feeds only on pine seeds. It uses its bill to reach the scales of pine cones, open them, and extract the pine nuts.

Exposed Legs

Taking a quick look at the extremities of birds, including their toes and claws, can help us learn about their behavior. The skin of their legs and feet can have some striking features. All these characteristics reveal information about the environments in which different groups of birds live, as well as about their diets. Scientists use these characteristics as a basis for classifying birds. The detailed study of the anatomy of a bird's leg and foot can offer useful information. The shape and placement of bones, muscles, and tendons make it possible to understand how birds hold their prey or perch on branches, as well as to learn about the mechanics of their movement across the ground and in the water.

Different Types

The foot usually has four toes. Three of them have a similar size and position. Opposite them is a smaller toe called the hallux. This pattern varies among different bird groups. For example, the position and shape of toes can differ. There are even cases in which two toes are functional while the others have been reduced in size. This is the case with flightless birds such as rheas. Differences are also found in the skin, which may form a web between the toes and projections of horn. All these characteristics become tools to help the bird survive in its environment and face challenges regarding obtaining food.

FEET DESIGNED FOR SEIZING
Found on birds of prey and nocturnal rapacious birds. Their feet are strong, and their toes end in long, curved, sharp claws. They seize prey and transport it in flight.

FEET DESIGNED FOR WALKING
Found on herons, flamingos, and storks. The toes and legs are very long. The hallux is pointed backward. They live in places with soft ground, such as swamps and river banks.

FEET DESIGNED FOR SWIMMING
Found on auks, ducks, and penguins, which have a membrane between their toes that forms a web and increases the surface of the foot that is in contact with the water.

FEET DESIGNED FOR CLIMBING
Found on parrots, woodpeckers, and cuckoos. The hallux and the fourth toe are pointed backward. This arrangement provides the birds with more strength for climbing tree trunks.

FEET DESIGNED FOR PERCHING
Found on hummingbirds, kingfishers, ovenbirds, and nightjars. They have small feet, with the second, third, and fourth toes joined together. This makes it possible for them to stand still.

FEET DESIGNED FOR RUNNING
Found on bustards, curlews, and rheas. They have long legs with short toes. The hallux and the fourth toe are very small, which decreases contact with the ground while running.

THE FOOT II
The distal tarsal bones merge into the metatarsal bone and create tarsometatarsal bones.

THE FOOT I
Toes 1 (hallux) and 2 have three phalanges, toe 3 has four, and toe 4 has five.

3 4   2   1

Adaptation to Trees
The common waxbill perches and sleeps on tree branches without expending much energy. The weight of the body alone causes its toes to close tightly around the branch.

TRICOLORED HERON
Its feet have long, thin toes that allow it to move on soft ground, such as in swamps, on river banks, and on lake shores. It lives in the regions of Arica and Coquimbo in Chile.

Claws, Scales, and Spurs

These striking foot structures play a role in finding food, movement, protection, and defense, among other things. The claws can be long and sharp, in the case of birds of prey, or short and round, in the case of walking birds. Owls have a comblike claw that they use to groom their plumage. Their scales, inherited from reptiles, help protect their feet. In some cases, they help the birds to move through water. Many birds, such as chickens, pheasants, and crested screamers (a South American waterbird), have a spur, which they can use as a weapon.

BALD EAGLE
(Talons)
Very long, curved, pointed claws. They envelop the body of the prey and pierce it.

KNEE AND THIGH
The thigh is included in the body and has a shortened femur. The knee is near the center of gravity.

GREAT CRESTED GREBE (Lobed Toes)
In some swimming birds, the toes look like oars. They have a continuous wide border.

TIBIA
The tibia merges into tarsal bones and forms the tibiotarsus. It has a slightly developed fibula on its lateral face.

BIRD LEG

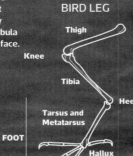

Thigh
Knee
Tibia
Heel
Tarsus and Metatarsus
FOOT
Hallux
Toes

HUMAN LEG

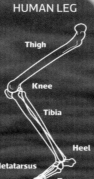

Thigh
Knee
Tibia
Heel
Metatarsus
Toes
Tarsus
Foot

ANKLE
Also known as a false knee because it looks like a knee that flexes backward.

SCOTS DUMPY ROOSTER (Spurs)
The spurs originate in skin and bone tissues. When males fight over territory or over a female, they use their spurs to defend themselves.

Internal/External Structure

Birds walk on their toes, which form the first portion of their feet. The second portion is formed by the tarsometatarsus. Its top part is connected to the tibia, through a joint similar to that of our ankle. That is why the leg flexes backward. The knee, similar to ours, is higher up and works like a hip. It is located close to the body, and it helps to maintain balance. The thigh bone also stabilizes the body by adding weight to the skeleton. All the movements of these bones are controlled by tendons and muscles.

The Art of Flying

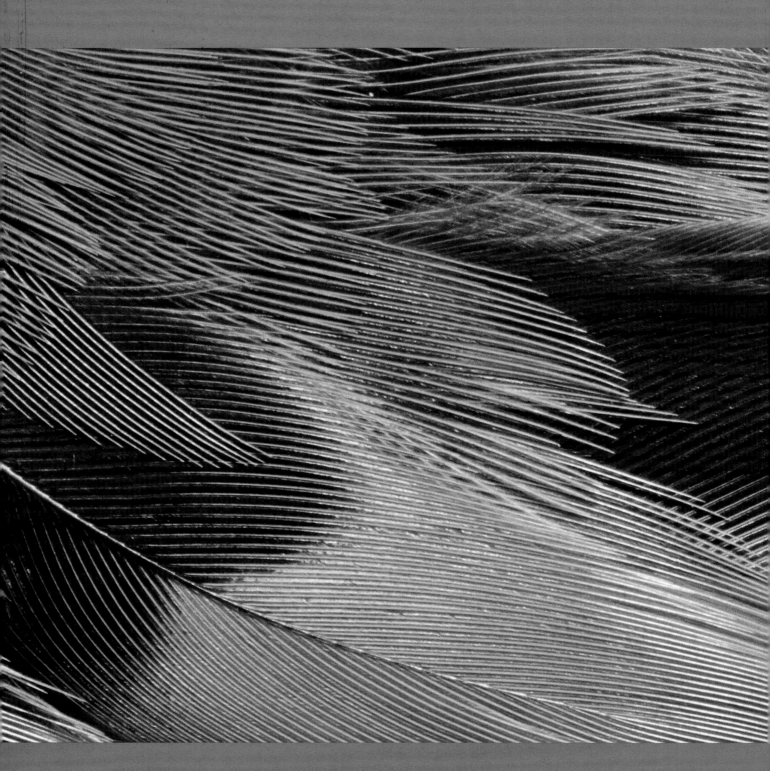

Birds move in the air the same way a glider does, that is, by making the most of air currents to gain height and speed while moving. The shape of the wings varies according to the needs of each bird group. Some cover considerable distances and thus have long, narrow wings, whereas others have short, rounded

PARROT FEATHER
Detail of the feathers worn by
these colorful aerial acrobats.

wings that allow them to make short flights from branch to branch. Birds also have shiny, colorful feathers that males frequently use both to attract females and to hide from enemies.

Feathers are usually renewed once a year, and this process is as vital to birds as feeding. ●

Adaptations

There are three main theories to explain why birds developed the ability to fly. The evidence that supports each of them tells a story of adaptations to an aerial world in which the fight for food and survival is key. One reasonable theory argues that birds descended from an extinct line of biped reptiles that fed on plants and used to jump from branch to branch to flee. ●

Today

The tips of the wings propel flight; the arms support the bird; and the shoulders enable the flapping movements.

From Reptile to Bird

It is known that several evolutionary lineages from both reptiles and birds did not survive the evolutionary process, and that the lineage that truly links these two animal groups has not yet been found. However, some theories state that the change from reptile to bird took place through a long process of adaptation. There are two arguments and a variant: the arboreal theory, which posits an air-ground flight model; the cursory (or running) theory, which focuses on the need for stability when running; and a variant, related to parental care, which posits that dinosaurs started to fly as a way of keeping their eggs safe.

1 THE ARBOREAL THEORY

This theory, the most accepted for a long time, states that flight was an adaptation to the environment in which certain herbivorous climbing reptiles lived. At first, dinosaurs developed a kind of parachute to protect them if they missed a branch when jumping, and later it became a way to move from tree to tree. Finally, flight evolved to involve the flapping of wings, which allowed the animal to cover greater distances.

GLIDING
Flight made it possible to move from tree to tree without using the ground.

FLAPPING
Gliding was improved to cover distances and increase agility.

CLIMBING
The evolution of dinosaurs yielded climbing species.

JUMPING
Adapted to aerial life, they jumped from branch to branch.

2 THE CURSORY, OR RUNNING, THEORY

Supported by good fossil evidence, the running theory argues that birds descended from certain bipedal dinosaurs that were fast runners. Their arms opened, evolving into wings, to stabilize them as they jumped. Progression from this development to flying was simply a matter of time.

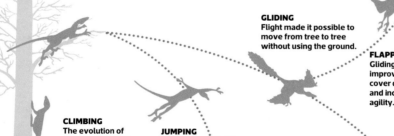

JUMPING
As they jumped high, their wings stabilized them, allowing them to catch prey.

RUNNING
Their two legs enabled them to run at high speeds.

FLAPPING
After developing the ability to jump and glide, these reptiles started flapping to cover greater distances.

3 PARENTAL CARE VARIANT

This variant proposes that reptiles started to climb trees to prevent their young from becoming prey. Gliding removed the need to climb out of the trees.

150 MILLION YEARS AGO
The bones are extended and reinforced; then they merge.

Highly Mobile Shoulder

Emergence of the Tarsometatarsus

175 MILLION YEARS AGO
The shoulders can perform a wider range of movements. The fingers merge.

Rotary Shoulder

Three Fingers

200 MILLION YEARS AGO
Dinosaur arm with pincer claw and limited movement

Limited Shoulder

Five Fingers

Short Arm

THE EMERGENCE OF THE WING
It evolved from an arm with a talon into a limb, without a talon, that was adapted for flight. The causes of this change are not yet clear to scientists. However, fossil records show how bones merged until they reached their present forms.

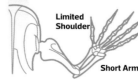

GLIDING SPECIES

Flying
Squirrel

Flying
Gecko

OTHER FLYING ANIMALS

In flying animals, from primitive pterodactyls to bats, wings have always been a flap of skin. A tear creates serious problems because it takes time to heal, and the wing may be misshapen afterward.

THE BEST SOLUTION

Feathers are a unique evolutionary advantage. Their versatility, strength, individual nature, and ease of replacement make them an ideal adaptation to flight for vertebrates.

FEATHERS

4 Today found only on birds, feathers are scales partitioned into three smaller sections. They form a light, uniform, resistant network that covers the whole body.

26 pounds (12 kg)

IS THE MAXIMUM WEIGHT AN EAGLE CAN CARRY DURING FLIGHT.

The eagle itself usually weighs about 13 pounds (6 kg) and can generally carry prey weighing 6.5 pounds (3 kg). Some eagles, however, have been seen carrying prey estimated to weigh 13 pounds (6 kg). Carrying any more weight would require bigger wings, which would be more difficult to move and less efficient. It is believed that large flying animals disappeared because of this limitation.

3 MODIFIED SCALES
They became divided into smaller sections.

2 LARGE SCALES
Several dinosaur species had them.

1 SCALES
Resistant, they covered the body of dinosaurs.

EAGLE

In its maneuvers, this great hunter displays the entire evolution of flight.

FROM SCALES TO FEATHERS

Feathers evolved from scales, and they are made of the same material. Feathers keep the body's temperature constant and are lighter than scales.

Feathers

Feathers distinguish birds from all other animals. They make birds strikingly colorful, protect them against cold and intense heat, enable them to move easily through the air and water, and hide them from enemies. Feathers are also one of the reasons why human beings have domesticated, caught, and hunted birds. A bird's set of feathers is called its plumage, and its color is essential for reproductive success. ●

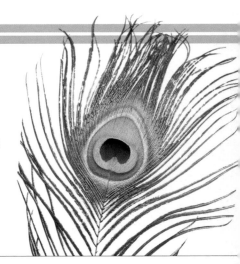

Structure

The structure of feathers has two parts: a shaft and a blade. The shaft is called the rachis, and the part connected to the bird's skin is called the calamus. The movement of a feather is generated in the rachis. The blade is composed of barbs that branch into barbules. The feather's blade, in which the barbules have a series of barbicels, or hooklets, at the tip, is called a vane. The interlocking hooklets in the vane create a network that adds rigidity and resistance to the feather. It also defines the characteristic aerodynamic shape of feathers and helps make the feather waterproof. When feathers wear out, birds have the ability to replace them with new ones.

1 A swelling, or papilla, develops in the bird's skin.

2 In the papilla, special skin cells form a follicle.

3 A tube that will extend from its base and become a feather grows in the follicle.

EDGE
The edge presents an excellent aerodynamic profile for flying.

RACHIS
A feather's main shaft, similar to a hollow rod

HOLLOW INTERIOR

INNER PULP OF THE SHAFT

INFERIOR UMBILICUS
The orifice at the base of the calamus, into which the dermic papilla penetrates. New feathers receive nourishment through it.

CALAMUS
It provides the necessary nutrients for feathers to grow. Nerve endings that stimulate the feather's movement are found at its base. This allows the bird to detect changes in its surroundings.

SUPERIOR UMBILICUS
It contains some loose barbs. Some feathers have a secondary rachis, the hyporachis.

BARBS
They are slim, straight ramifications that grow perpendicular to the rachis.

Types of Feathers

There are three main types of feathers, classified according to placement: those closest to the body are down, or underlying feathers; those at the top are contour feathers; and those on the wings and tail are flight feathers, which are often referred to as remiges (on the wings) and rectrices (on the tail).

DOWN

These light and silky feathers protect the bird against the cold. They have a short rachis, or none at all. Their barbs are long, and their barbules lack hooklets. In general, down is the first type of feather that birds develop when they hatch.

CONTOUR

Also called covert feathers, contours are short and rounded. They are more rigid than down feathers. Because they cover the body, wings, and tail, they give birds their shape as they fly.

WHAT IS KERATIN?

Keratin is a protein that forms part of the outermost layer of a bird's skin, just as it does in other vertebrate animal groups. Keratin is the main component of feathers, hair, and scales. Its distinct resistance helps keep the hooklets woven together in the vane. This allows birds' feathers to maintain their shape in spite of the pressure exerted by the air during flight.

BARBS

BARBULES

HOOKLETS, OR BARBICELS

VANE, OR BLADE
Its outer portion contains a great number of barbicels.

25,000

THE NUMBER OF FEATHERS THAT LARGE BIRDS, SUCH AS SWANS, CAN HAVE.
In contrast, the number of feathers small birds, such as songbirds, can have varies between 2,000 and 4,000.

TRAILING EDGE NOTCH
The turbulence during flight is reduced by this notch, found near the tip of the wing.

PREENING THE PLUMAGE

Birds need to preen their feathers with their bills not only to keep them clean and free of parasites but also to keep them lubricated, which helps birds resist inclement weather. Birds touch their uropygial, or preen, glands with their bills. Then they distribute the oil and wax this gland produces all over their plumage. This task is a matter of survival.

SELF-CLEANING WITH ANTS

Some birds, such as certain tanagers, catch ants with their bills and grind them. They then oil their feathers with the ground-up ants. It is believed that the acid juices from the squashed ants work as a repellent against lice and other external parasites.

DUST BATH

Birds such as pheasants, partridges, ostriches, pigeons, and sparrows perform dust baths to control the amount of grease on their feathers.

PTERYLAE AND APTERIA

At first glance, a bird's body is covered with feathers. However, feathers do not grow all over the body but rather in particular areas called pterylae. This is where the papillae, which create new feathers, are found. The shape and placement of pterylae vary according to species. Pterylae are surrounded by naked areas, called apteria, in which feathers do not grow. Penguins are the only birds whose bodies are completely covered with feathers. This characteristic makes it possible for them to live in cold regions.

IMPERIAL HERON
Powder down keeps its plumage waterproof.

SPECIAL FEATHERS

Vibrissae are special feathers formed by only one filament. Sometimes they have loose barbs at the base that perform a tactile function. They are located at the base of bills or nostrils or around the eyes. They are very thin and are usually blended with contour feathers.

Vibrissae

Filoplumes

POWDER DOWN

This special type of feather can be found on some aquatic birds. They grow constantly and break off at the tip into small waxy scales. This "powder" is preened into the plumage to provide protection.

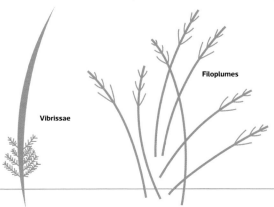

Wings to Fly

Wings are highly modified arms that, through their unique structure and shape, enable most birds to fly. There are many types of wings that vary by species. For instance, penguins, which are flightless, use their wings for the specialized task of swimming. Among all wings that have existed in the animal kingdom, those of birds are the best for flying. Their wings are light and durable, and in some cases, their shape and effectiveness can be modified during flight. To understand the relationship between wings and a bird's weight, the concept of wing loading, which helps explain the type of flight for each species, is useful.

Wings in the Animal Kingdom

Wings have always been modified arms, from the first models on pterosaurs to those on modern birds. Wings have evolved, beginning with the adaptation of bones. Non-avian wings have a membranous surface composed of flexible skin. They extend from the bones of the hand and body usually down to the legs, depending on the species. Avian wings, on the other hand, are based on a very different principle: the arm and hand form a complex of skin, bone, and muscle, with a wing surface consisting of feathers. Furthermore, the avian wing allows for important changes in form, depending on the bird's adaptation to the environment.

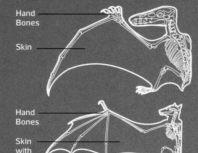

Hand Bones
Skin

PTERODACTYLS still had talons, and only one finger extended their wings.

Hand Bones
Skin with Hair

BATS Four fingers extend the membrane, and the thumb remains as a talon.

Hand Bones
Feathers

BIRDS The fused fingers form the tip of the wing where the rectrices, or primary feathers, are attached.

Types of Wings

According to the environment in which they live and the type of flight they perform, birds have different wing shapes that allow them to save energy and to perform efficiently during flight. The wing shape also depends on the bird's size. Consequently, the number of primary and secondary feathers changes depending on the needs of a given species.

The external primary feathers are longer.

The outermost primary feathers are shorter than the central ones.

They are wide at the base, with separate feather tips.

There are many secondary feathers.

Short feathers are located all over the wing.

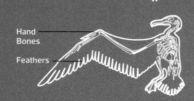

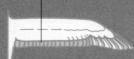

FAST WING
Remiges are large and tight to allow for flapping; the surface is reduced to prevent excessive friction.

ELLIPTICAL WINGS
Functional for mixed flights, they are very maneuverable. Many birds have them.

WINGS FOR SOARING ABOVE LAND
Wide, they are used to fly at low speeds. The separate remiges prevent turbulence when gliding.

WINGS FOR SOARING ABOVE THE OCEAN
Their great length and small width make them ideal for gliding against the wind, as flying requires.

WINGS FOR SWIMMING
In adapting to swimming, the feathers of penguins became short, and they serve primarily as insulation.

Wing Size and Loading

The wingspan is the distance between the tips of the wings. Together with width, it determines the surface area, which is an essential measurement for bird flight. Not just any wing can support any bird. There is a close relationship between the animal's size (measured by weight) and the surface area of its wings. This relationship is called wing loading, and it is crucial in understanding the flight of certain species. Albatrosses, with large wings, have low wing loading, which makes them great gliders, whereas hummingbirds have to flap their small wings intensely to support their own weight. The smaller the wing loading, the more a bird can glide; the bigger, the faster a bird can fly.

11.5 ft
(3.5 m)

WANDERING ALBATROSS

5 ft
(1.5 m)

24 ft
(7.3 m)

ARGENTAVIS MAGNIFICENS
(extinct)

LARGER FINGER

SMALLER FINGER

CARPOMETACARPUS

ALULAR DIGIT
Controls the alula, a feathered projection on the front edge of the wing.

ULNA

RADIUS

HUMERUS

CORACOID

STERNUM OR KEEL

PRIMARIES
They are in charge of propulsion; they are also called remiges.

PRIMARY COVERTS
They cover the remiges and, with the alula, change the wing shape at will.

MEDIAN WING COVERTS
They change the wing's lift when they rise slightly.

SECONDARIES
Their number varies greatly depending on the species. They complete the surface.

GREATER WING COVERTS
They create more surface area and cover the intersection point of the tertiaries.

TERTIARIES
Together with the secondaries, they create the wing's surface.

LOOSE FEATHERS
Sometimes barbicels are missing, and feathers on the wing come apart, creating a loose and ruffled appearance.

PRIMARY FEATHERS
Flying birds have from nine to 12 primary feathers. Running birds may have up to 16.

Flightless Wings

Among these, penguins' wings are an extreme case of adaptation: designed for rowing underwater, they work as fins. On running birds, wings' first and foremost function is to provide balance as the bird runs. These wings are also related to courtship, as birds show off their ornamental feathers during mating season by opening their wings or flapping them. Wings are also very efficient at controlling temperature, as birds use them as fans to ventilate their bodies.

FUNCTION
The wings of ostriches carry out the functions of balancing, temperature regulation, and courtship.

Tail Types

O ver the course of evolution, birds' tail vertebrae fused into a pygostyle, and in their place, feathers of different sizes and colors emerged. These feathers have multiple uses: they can control aerial maneuvers during flight, work as brakes during landing, and make noise. Males also use them during courtship to dazzle and win over females. Usually the tail is formed by rectrices that vary in number, length, and rigidity depending on the species.

① ② ③

The Key to How It Works

➡ The tail can perform a variety of functions because of the movement and shape of the feathers. The powerful muscles in the pygostyle prepare the plumage for courtship displays and for flight, provide balance in walking and alighting on trees, and work as rudders for swimming.

OPEN	CLOSED	OPEN

LANDING I
The plumage spreads out, and the main axis of the body is positioned parallel to the ground.

LANDING II
The body leans backward, and the tail closes. The legs prepare to grab the branch.

LANDING III
The spread-out tail feathers, together with an intense flapping of the wings, make it possible for the bird to slow down and prepare its body to land.

Courtship Display

The tail feathers of the female black grouse are straight, whereas those of the male have a half-moon shape. They usually keep the feathers closed and near the ground, but during the courtship displays they spread them out and show them off completely. To finish the show, the male runs back and forth in front of the female.

OPEN   CLOSED

RECTRICES
Tail feathers can wear out and fray because of friction during flight or by brushing against vegetation.

UNDERTAIL COVERTS
Feathers that cover the lower part of rectrices, protecting them against the wear and tear caused by air friction

Black Grouse
Lyrurus tetrix

The male is recognized by its bluish black plumage and the red caruncle over its eyes.

Fan of Rectrices

On flying birds, it is light and aerodynamic. On tree-climbing birds, such as woodpeckers, the plumage is rigid, which allows them to use it as a support (pointed tail). The coverts of male peacocks are more developed than their rectrices so that the peacock can show them off.

FORKED TAIL
Found on swallows and frigate birds. The external feathers are very long and look like scissors.

ROUNDED TAIL
Found on some songbirds. The central feathers are only slightly longer than the external ones.

GRADUATED TAIL
Found on trogons and kingfishers. When closed, the tail has a layered shape.

MARGINATED TAIL
Found on blue jays. The central feathers are only slightly shorter than the external ones.

SQUARE TAIL
Found on quails. The tail is short, with even-sized feathers.

To Renew Is to Live

The periodic renewal of plumage is called molting. It is the replacement of worn-out, older feathers with new ones that are in better condition. In a bird's life cycle, molting is as important an event as migrating or caring for young. The beginning of this phenomenon is determined by environmental factors that trigger a series of hormonal stimuli in birds: they start to eat more and to decrease their other activities. This, in turn, causes them to gain weight through an accumulation of fat that will serve as the source of energy for developing new plumage. ●

Plumage Molting

The main function of molting is to replace worn-out plumage. It also helps the bird adapt its appearance to the seasons and to different stages in life. The renewal can be partial or total. Some feathers are replaced before the spring, when the task is to attract a partner for reproductive purposes. In the fall, before birds have to start caring for their young, the renewal is complete. On most birds, molting takes place in each pteryla, following a determined order. Penguins, however, renew all their feathers at the same time, within two to six weeks.

SEASONAL CHANGE

In the high mountains, snow transforms the landscape during winter. During this time, nonmigratory birds exchange their summer plumage for a winter one. This change helps them to protect themselves from predators.

PTARMIGAN

SUMMER PLUMAGE
The feathers have deep pigmentation. This helps birds blend in with the vegetation.

WINTER PLUMAGE
The new, unpigmented feathers make it possible for ptarmigans to blend with the white snow.

OLD FEATHER
Renewing the plumage is important because it helps keep the bird's body temperature stable. It also keeps the feathers in place while the bird moves about, and it helps the bird to go unnoticed by predators.

DERMAL PAPILLAE
A feather develops in each of them.

DERMIS

FOLLICLE   EPIDERMIS

NEW FEATHER BEING FORMED

1
In the epidermal papilla, the formation of the new feather causes the detachment of the worn-out one.

2
A papilla develops from skin cells. The epidermal cells multiply faster than the dermal ones and form a collar-shaped depression called the follicle.

Order of Replacement

Many species start molting, a process triggered by hormones, in a specific order. Molting starts with remiges and wing coverts, continues with rectrices, and finishes with body coverts. This gradual process keeps the body temperature stable.

SCAPULARS

ALULAE

COVERTS

SECONDARY REMIGES

PRIMARY REMIGES

RECTRICES

4 Massive replacement of chest, back, and head coverts occurs from the center outward. This change coincides with the substitution of the seventh remex (singular of *remiges*).

3 Rectrices are replaced from the center outward. This happens simultaneously with the loss of tertiary remiges.

2 The wing coverts are replaced.

1 Renewal starts in the first primary remiges and spreads outward. In the secondary remiges, it spreads in two directions. Replacement occurs when the new remiges are three fourths developed.

61%

THE PERCENTAGE OF A BIRD'S BODY COVERED BY FEATHERS WHEN RENEWAL IS AT ITS PEAK

DEVELOPING PLUMAGE

BLOOD VESSELS **nourish the feathers during their development.**

DEVELOPING BARBS

VANE

BARBS

NEW FEATHER

EPIDERMAL COLLAR

3 The papilla grows and becomes layered. The outermost layer is covered with keratin, which protects the underlying Malpighian layer (nucleus of the papilla). A group of dermal cells brings nutrients through the blood vessels that travel along the new feather.

4 The rapid growth of the Malpighian layer starts to develop the new feather. The rachis, barbs, and barbules become keratinized. The vessels that bring nutrients are reabsorbed, and the connection with the dermic layer is closed. Finally the protective vane breaks, and the feather unfurls.

5 The feather, now lifeless, assumes its characteristic blade shape. A residue of dermal and epidermal cells at the base of the follicle forms an area that will allow for replacement when the feather wears out.

20 days

IS THE AVERAGE AMOUNT OF TIME THAT IT TAKES FOR A NEW FEATHER TO FORM.

Gliding

Gliding involves using air currents to fly and save energy when traveling long distances. There are two types of gliders, terrestrial birds and marine birds, each of which is adapted to different atmospheric phenomena. Terrestrial birds rise on thermals (rising air currents). Marine birds make use of oceanic surface winds. Once the birds gain altitude, they glide off in straight paths. They slowly lose altitude until encountering another thermal that will lift them. Both terrestrial and marine gliders have wings of considerable size. ●

TYPES OF GLIDING FEATHERS

Terrestrial Glider
A large wing surface allows it to make the most of rising air currents at moderate speed.

Marine Glider
Thin and long wings allow it to make the most of the constant surface winds and offer less resistance to forward movement.

Takeoff

Usually, a powerful jump followed by the vertical flapping of the wings is enough to make a bird take flight. As it descends, the tip feathers are stacked on top of each other, forming an airtight surface that helps drive the bird upward. As the bird raises its wings to repeat the movement, the feathers curve and open until the wing reaches its highest point. With a couple of flaps of the wings, the bird is in flight. Bigger birds need a running start on the ground or water in order to take off.

2. During the downward movement, the primary feathers are closed, which prevents air from passing through.

Air

3. Ascent

Fast and Strong Flapping

1. During the upward movement in wing flapping, the primary feathers open up, offering less resistance to the air.

Initial Jump

Run

70%
THE ENERGY SAVED BY A SEAGULL WHILE GLIDING

SECONDARY FEATHERS
There are many of these because of the wing's length.

The wing length of some pelicans may reach 8 feet (240 cm) from tip to tip.

PRIMARY FEATHERS
There are fewer of these, as they only form the tip.

MOVING FORWARD

CONTINUOUS AIR

WINGLETS

Terrestrial gliders usually have separate primary feathers (toward the tip of the wing) that serve to decrease the noise and tension generated there by the passing of air. Modern airplanes copy their design.

The tip feathers work as airplane winglets.

Airplane Winglets are made of one or several pieces.

Marine Birds

Dynamic soaring is performed by birds with long and thin wings, such as the albatross. These wings are designed to take advantage of horizontal air currents, which are responsible for the formation of waves in the ocean. The result is a flight consisting of a series of loops as the bird is lifted upward when it faces the wind and moved forward when it faces away from the wind. This kind of flight can be performed at any time.

WEAKER WIND

STRONGER WIND

Dynamic soaring allows birds to cover long distances in the direction they desire.

3 to 33 feet (1–10 m) is the range in altitude for dynamic soaring.

FLIGHT PATTERNS

Flying in formation is a way for birds in flapping flight to save energy. The leader encounters more resistance as it flies, while the others take advantage of its wake. There are two basic patterns: "L" and "V." The first is used by pelicans, and the second is used by geese.

Relay
When the leader gets tired, another bird takes its position.

14%

THE PERCENTAGE OF WING FLAPPING THAT GEESE SPARE THEMSELVES BY FLYING IN FORMATION

"L" FORMATION
Leader
The leader makes the most effort, as it "parts" the air.

The Rest of the Formation
The other birds make use of the turbulence produced by the leader's flapping to gain height, following along behind.

"V" FORMATION
The principle is the same, but the birds form two lines that converge at a point. This is the usual formation used by geese, ducks, and herons.

SPEED OF DISPLACEMENT
depends on the strength of the headwind.

THE WING
Its particular shape causes lift, with its convex side and less pronounced concave side.

LIFT

FASTER AIRSTREAM

CONSTANT AIRSTREAM

PATAGIUM
Elastic and resistant skin covering with feathers. It is the wing's cutting edge, responsible for dividing the airstream.

UPPER SIDE
Convex. The air covers more distance and accelerates, causing a lower pressure that "sucks" the wing upward.

LOWER SIDE
Concave. The air covers less distance, it does not accelerate, and its pressure does not change.

1 Ascent
When birds find a warm air current, they gain height without having to flap their wings.

Thermal: Hot Air

2 Straight Gliding
Once the maximum possible height is gained, the birds glide in straight paths.

Cold Air

3 Descent
The birds slowly glide downward.

4 Ascent
They rise again when they encounter another warm air current.

Warm Air Current

TERRESTRIAL BIRDS
They use warm, rising air currents generated through convection in the atmosphere or through the deflection of air currents against crags or mountains. Then they glide in a straight flight path. This type of flight is possible only during the day.

Flapping Flight

Most flying birds use flapping flight all the time. This consists of moving through the air as if rowing with the wings. With each flap (raising and lowering), the wings both sustain the bird in the air and push its body forward. There are different types of flapping flight and different rates of flapping. In general, the larger the bird, the more powerful and less frequent its flapping will be. Because flapping is an activity that consumes much energy, birds have adapted a variety of flight patterns: some, like hummingbirds, always flap their wings, whereas others alternate flapping with short-term gliding. The wing shape also varies according to the bird's needs. Birds that cover long distances have long, narrow wings; those that fly among trees have short, rounded wings. ●

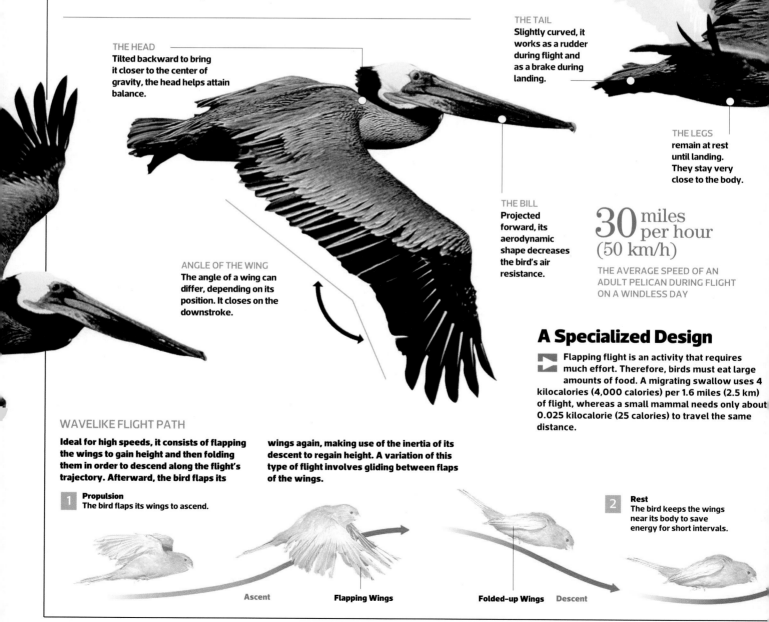

THE HEAD
Tilted backward to bring it closer to the center of gravity, the head helps attain balance.

THE TAIL
Slightly curved, it works as a rudder during flight and as a brake during landing.

THE LEGS
remain at rest until landing. They stay very close to the body.

THE BILL
Projected forward, its aerodynamic shape decreases the bird's air resistance.

ANGLE OF THE WING
The angle of a wing can differ, depending on its position. It closes on the downstroke.

30 miles per hour (50 km/h)
THE AVERAGE SPEED OF AN ADULT PELICAN DURING FLIGHT ON A WINDLESS DAY

A Specialized Design

Flapping flight is an activity that requires much effort. Therefore, birds must eat large amounts of food. A migrating swallow uses 4 kilocalories (4,000 calories) per 1.6 miles (2.5 km) of flight, whereas a small mammal needs only about 0.025 kilocalorie (25 calories) to travel the same distance.

WAVELIKE FLIGHT PATH

Ideal for high speeds, it consists of flapping the wings to gain height and then folding them in order to descend along the flight's trajectory. Afterward, the bird flaps its wings again, making use of the inertia of its descent to regain height. A variation of this type of flight involves gliding between flaps of the wings.

1 Propulsion
The bird flaps its wings to ascend.

2 Rest
The bird keeps the wings near its body to save energy for short intervals.

Ascent   Flapping Wings   Folded-up Wings   Descent

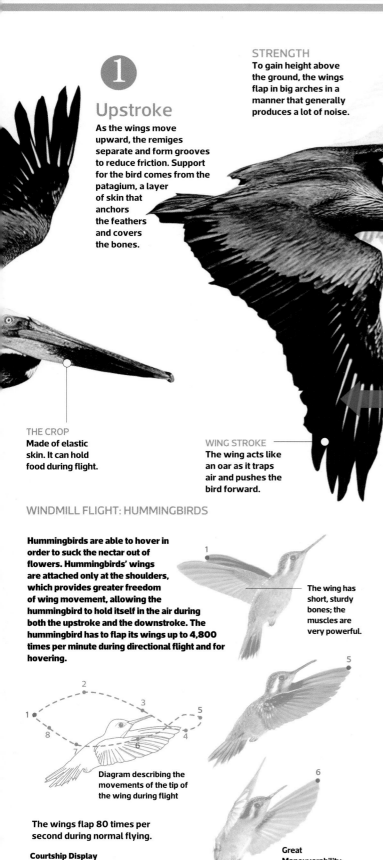

1 Upstroke

As the wings move upward, the remiges separate and form grooves to reduce friction. Support for the bird comes from the patagium, a layer of skin that anchors the feathers and covers the bones.

STRENGTH
To gain height above the ground, the wings flap in big arches in a manner that generally produces a lot of noise.

2 Downstroke

As the wings move downward, the remiges are forced together, and the wing moves forward a little for extra support. The wing also bends at the tips to push the bird forward, as if it were rowing.

Muscular strength is distributed to the entire wing, but it increases near the tip.

THE CROP
Made of elastic skin. It can hold food during flight.

WING STROKE
The wing acts like an oar as it traps air and pushes the bird forward.

The downstroke of the wing provides propulsion.

WINDMILL FLIGHT: HUMMINGBIRDS

Hummingbirds are able to hover in order to suck the nectar out of flowers. Hummingbirds' wings are attached only at the shoulders, which provides greater freedom of wing movement, allowing the hummingbird to hold itself in the air during both the upstroke and the downstroke. The hummingbird has to flap its wings up to 4,800 times per minute during directional flight and for hovering.

The wing has short, sturdy bones; the muscles are very powerful.

Diagram describing the movements of the tip of the wing during flight

The wings flap 80 times per second during normal flying.

Courtship Display
Certain hummingbird species can flap their wings up to 200 times per second during courtship.

Great Maneuverability:
Hummingbirds are the only birds capable of moving backward.

Landing

requires reducing speed until the bird becomes motionless and settles. The bird faces the wind and spreads out its tail, wings, and alulae (bastard wings, characterized by their stiffness and growth from the first digit), while lifting up its body and extending its legs forward to increase the surface area in contact with the air. In addition, the bird flaps its wings intensely in the direction opposite to its flight. Everything works like an aerodynamic brake. Some birds—such as the albatross, with its long, narrow wings—tend to have problems slowing down. As a result, they are ungainly when landing on the ground, but on the water they are able to ski on their feet until coming to a stop.

Flapping Against the Wind

Open Wings

WIND

Spread Tail

Sliding

The feet spread open before landing to provide more resistance and help the bird to slow down.

Speed Records

The world of birds is amazing when expressed in numbers. Most birds travel at speeds between 25 and 45 miles per hour (40–70 km/h), but when diving, peregrine falcons can reach more than 200 miles per hour (320 km/h). Many species can reach an altitude of 6,600 feet (2,000 m), although climbers have seen geese flying over the Himalayas at more than 26,000 feet (8,000 m). The fastest swimmer is the Gentoo penguin, which can swim 22.4 miles per hour (36 km/h). Considering its small size, it is surprising that the *Selasphorus rufus*, or Rufous hummingbird, which is only 4 inches (10 cm) long, carries out an extensive round-trip migration each year from northern Alaska to Mexico. Here are some more incredible facts. ●

Air

SPEED ▲

Most birds fly between 25 and 45 miles per hour (45 and 70 km/h), but the fastest birds can beat the cheetah, the most famous of the fast animals.

ALTITUDE ▲

Flying at high altitudes requires a strengthened circulatory system to make up for the scarcity of oxygen in the air.

RUPPELL'S GRIFFON VULTURE
36,870 feet (11,237 m)

In 1973 a Ruppell's griffon vulture crashed into an airplane flying over the Ivory Coast at this altitude.

Weight
15–20 pounds (7–9 kg)

Flying Altitude commonly reaches 20,000 feet (6,000 m).

Scale (in thousands of feet)

—— 7.9 ft (2.4 m) ——

CHOUGH
29,030 FEET (8,848 M)

A group of climbers on Mt. Everest found choughs standing on the summit.

BAR-HEADED GOOSE
28,000 FEET (8,500 M)

Some climbers reported having seen specimens of geese flying at 28,000 feet (8,500 m) over the Himalayas.

BLACK SWAN
27,000 FEET (8,230 M) OF ALTITUDE,
according to a pilot who witnessed a flock over the Hebrides Islands

EIDER
75 MPH (120 KM/H)

STARLING
38 MPH (60 KM/H)

DRAGONFLY
The fastest flying insect. It reaches
31 mph (50 km/h).

Scale (in miles per hour)

PARROT
24 MPH (38 KM/H)

PHEASANT
31 MPH (50 KM/H)

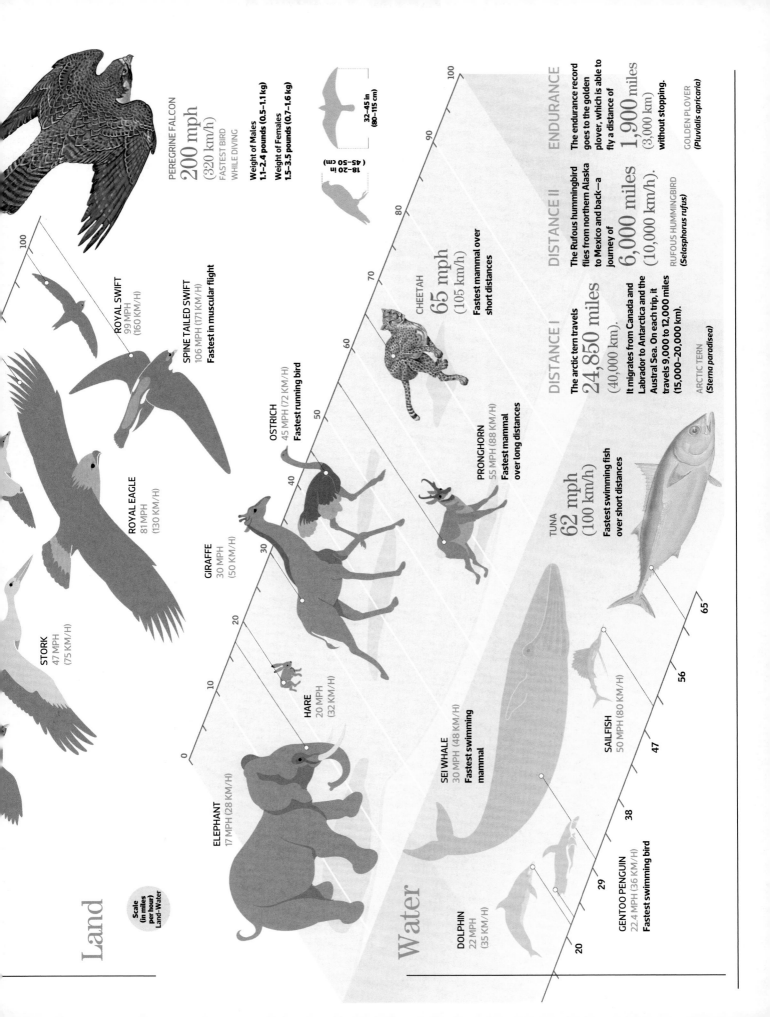

Land

Scale (in miles per hour) Land–Water

PEREGRINE FALCON
200 mph
(320 km/h)
FASTEST BIRD
WHILE DIVING

Weight of Males
1.1–2.4 pounds (0.5–1.1 kg)

Weight of Females
1.5–3.5 pounds (0.7–1.6 kg)

32–45 in
(80–115 cm)

18–20 in
(45–50 cm)

ROYAL SWIFT
99 MPH
(160 KM/H)

SPINE TAILED SWIFT
106 MPH (171KM/H)
Fastest in muscular flight

ROYAL EAGLE
81 MPH
(130 KM/H)

STORK
47 MPH
(75 KM/H)

OSTRICH
45 MPH (72 KM/H)
Fastest running bird

GIRAFFE
30 MPH
(50 KM/H)

HARE
20 MPH
(32 KM/H)

ELEPHANT
17 MPH (28 KM/H)

CHEETAH
65 mph
(105 km/h)
**Fastest mammal over
short distances**

PRONGHORN
55 MPH (88 KM/H)
**Fastest mammal
over long distances**

Water

DOLPHIN
22 MPH
(35 KM/H)

SEI WHALE
30 MPH (48 KM/H)
**Fastest swimming
mammal**

GENTOO PENGUIN
22.4 MPH (36 KM/H)
Fastest swimming bird

SAILFISH
50 MPH (80 KM/H)

TUNA
62 mph
(100 km/h)
**Fastest swimming fish
over short distances**

DISTANCE I

The arctic tern travels
24,850 miles
(40,000 km).

It migrates from Canada and
Labrador to Antarctica and the
Austral Sea. On each trip, it
travels 9,000 to 12,000 miles
(15,000–20,000 km).

ARCTIC TERN
(Sterna paradisea)

DISTANCE II

The Rufous hummingbird
flies from northern Alaska
to Mexico and back—a
journey of
6,000 miles
(10,000 km/h.)

RUFOUS HUMMINGBIRD
(Selasphorus rufus)

ENDURANCE

The endurance record
goes to the golden
plover, which is able to
fly a distance of
1,900 miles
(3,000 km)
without stopping.

GOLDEN PLOVER
(Pluvialis apricaria)

The Lives of Birds

The behavior of birds is closely connected to the seasons. To survive, birds must prepare for the arrival of fall and winter and adjust their behavior accordingly. Gliding over the oceans, a wandering albatross, for example, can travel anywhere from 1,800 to 9,300 miles (2,900 to 15,000 km) in a single day in search of food. When the time comes

PARTRIDGE EGGS (Lagopus lagopus scoticus)
The female lays eggs at intervals of one to two days, and she is the one who incubates them.

to choose a partner, the behavior of males is different from that of females: males employ a variety of tactics to win over females and convince them of their fitness. Some bird couples stay together forever, whereas other birds change partners every year. As for caring for chicks and building nests, in most species, both parents participate. ●

The Annual Cycle

The annual cycle of seasons is like the daily cycle of night and day. Fluctuations in the intensity of light over time create a series of physiological and behavioral changes in birds, whether throughout the year or throughout the day. This biological clock is clearly reflected in birds' reproduction and migrations. Changes in light that are detected by a bird's retinas induce the secretion of melatonin by the pineal gland. The blood level of this hormone acts on the hypothalamus–hypophysis axis, which regulates internal processes. This is one reason why birds start to change their plumage and feel the need to fly to other areas. ●

How the Hypophysis Works

Reproduction is the main activity under the control of the hypophysis, which determines behaviors such as finding a place to court females and mate, building a nest, incubating the eggs, and stimulating unborn chicks to break their shells. The hypophysis is a gland in the brain that has several functions. It receives nervous and chemical stimuli and produces hormones. These hormones regulate the metabolic activities that cause birds' internal and external sexual organs to develop. For example, the gonads become enlarged, and secondary sexual characteristics, such as ornamental crests or plumes, appear.

DORSAL VIEW

VENTRAL VIEW

ENLARGED AREA

- Olfactory
- Cerebral Hemisphere
- Optical Chiasm
- Optical Lobe
- Hypothalamus
- Cerebellum
- Medulla Oblongata
- Infundibulum and Hypophysis

Sleep Regulator
The pineal gland, or epiphysis, produces melatonin. The level of this hormone determines the phases of sleep and wakefulness.

THE MOST IMPORTANT GLAND
The hypophysis is located in the ventral area of the brain, below the hypothalamus. Its secretions control vital functions, from blood pressure and the balance of water and salts in the body to the activity of the gonads and the thyroid.

ANNUAL CYCLE
Incubation, migration, and courtship activities vary according to the amount of light available during each season.

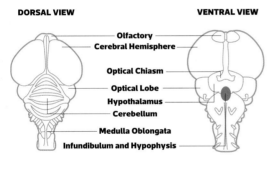

+ LIGHT

1

SUN

In early summer, incubation takes place. The increase in the amount of daylight coincides with this phase of the annual cycle.

2 The arrival of the first days of fall coincides with a decrease in the amount of light. The migration season begins.

- LIGHT

Survival Manual

Birds' most striking behaviors are associated with the reproductive season. During courtship parades, birds engage in elaborate choreographies; there are also extraordinary fights between males. The blue-footed booby, the male frigate bird, and the ruff are just a few examples of birds that engage in these behaviors. Others, such as the snowy egret *(Egretta thula)*, prefer to offer twigs for the construction of the nest. The Vogelkop bowerbird *(Amblyornis inornata)* builds bowers with leaves, flowers, or any other object that may help him to win over the female. Birds' performances are not connected only to courtship. The killdeer *(Charadrius vociferus)* fakes being wounded to defend the eggs or chicks in the nest from predators. It offers itself as easy prey by dragging a wing as if it were broken. This trick shifts the danger away from the young.

SHOWING OFF

The magnificent frigate bird *(Fregata magnificens)* is a large bird that lives in coastal areas. It has large wings, powerful talons, and a strong hooked bill. During the reproductive season, it is responsible for building the nest. With its impressive appearance, it endeavors to attract a female.

New House
While it prepares the nest, its chest rests, with its skin pink and relaxed.

Red Chest
The throat pouch remains inflated for several hours or until the female chooses the most seductive male.

Indicating Repose
To rest, the pelican reclines its head and places its bill under a wing.

DANCE OF THE BLUE-FOOTED BOOBY

(Sula nebouxii) The males—and, on occasion, the females—perform a graceful courtship dance after marking the territory for nesting. They sing and show off their plumage with careful synchronization.

1 Raised Head
It flaps its wings and marches, looking at the sky.

2 Parade
It lowers its head and parades like a soldier around the nest. Finally, it shakes its whole body.

IN COMBAT

In the summer, male ruffs develop a huge "ruff" and auricular feathers around their necks. Their courtships are violent and striking. When competing for mating territory, they struggle fiercely. Afterward, they docilely sprawl their bodies on the ground until the female chooses the lucky one.

Male Ruff
Philomachus pugnax

3 +LIGHT

The amount of light increases with the beginning of spring; males use their huge throat pouches to court females.

TO THE ORGANS

How They Communicate

Sound is an important form of expression in the lives of birds. Birds' sounds can be of two types: calls and songs. The former have a simple acoustic structure, with few notes. They are associated with coordinating the activities of a group, establishing communication between parents and their young, and maintaining contact between birds during migration. Songs, on the other hand, are more complex in rhythm and modulation. They are controlled by the sex hormones, primarily the male hormones. For this reason, males produce the most varied melodies. Songs are linked to sexual behavior and territorial defense. In general, birds either inherit or learn them.

 THE SONG AND THE BRAIN
Birds have a brain that is well developed for this function. Testosterone acts on the upper vocal center of the brain, which is in charge of memorizing, identifying, and transmitting the orders for the execution of the song.

 EXPULSION OF AIR TO THE BRONCHI
The air stored in the air sacs and lungs is expelled. As it passes through the syrinx (located between the bronchi and the trachea), it vibrates the tympaniform membranes. These membranes are the equivalent of vocal cords in humans.

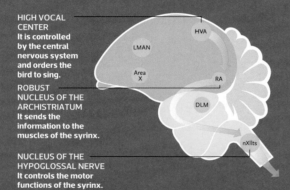

HIGH VOCAL CENTER
It is controlled by the central nervous system and orders the bird to sing.

ROBUST NUCLEUS OF THE ARCHISTRIATUM
It sends the information to the muscles of the syrinx.

NUCLEUS OF THE HYPOGLOSSAL NERVE
It controls the motor functions of the syrinx.

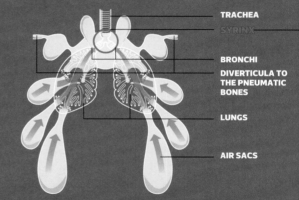

TRACHEA
SYRINX
BRONCHI
DIVERTICULA TO THE PNEUMATIC BONES
LUNGS
AIR SACS

 THE PRODUCTION OF SOUND IN THE SYRINX
The participation of both the sternotracheal muscles and five to seven pairs of small internal muscles is needed for producing sounds. These muscles control the elongation and contraction of the syrinx, which varies the pitch of the sound. The air sac is also important because it adds external pressure, which causes the tympaniform membranes to tighten. The esophagus works like a resonating box, amplifying the sound. The articulation of the sounds occurs in the buccopharyngeal cavity. There are two types of articulation: guttural and lingual.

SIMPLE SYRINX
The tympaniform membranes are located above the place where the bronchi divide. They are moved by a pair of external muscles.

TRACHEA
SOUND
VIBRATION OF THE WALL
MUSCULAR ACTION
TYMPANIFORM MEMBRANE
BRONCHIAL RINGS

SONG-PRODUCING SYRINX

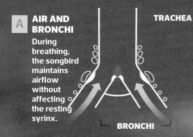

A AIR AND BRONCHI
During breathing, the songbird maintains airflow without affecting the resting syrinx.
TRACHEA
BRONCHI

B CLOSED MEMBRANE
The membranes close on both sides, under pressure from the external muscles. The bronchi rise slightly and also adjust the membranes.
PESSULUS
MUSCULAR ACTION
BRONCHIAL RINGS

C THE SOUND
The membranes vibrate with the air current and propagate the sound through the trachea until it reaches the bird's bill.
Tympaniform Membrane

Territoriality and Range

One of the most studied functions of birds' songs is territorial demarcation. When a bird occupies a territory, it sings to announce its claim to competitors, as the pipit shown to the left is doing. When birds must share territory, as in a colony, they develop dialects (variations of sounds produced by the species). When a bird born and raised in one location moves, it must learn the dialect of the new location in order to be accepted and participate in the community. There are also mechanical sounds produced by wing strokes, legs, and bills. In a display of territorial defense, the eared nightjar combines singing with beating its wings.

4,000 bird species

SHARE WITH HUMAN BEINGS AND WHALES THE NEED FOR "SOMEBODY" TO TEACH THEM TO VOCALIZE (SONGBIRDS, HUMMINGBIRDS, AND PARROTS ARE EXAMPLES).

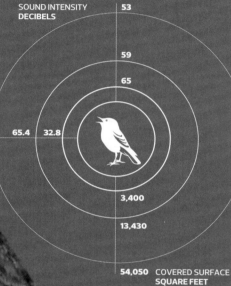

SOUND INTENSITY
DECIBELS

53
59
65

DISTANCE FEET 131.2 65.4 32.8

3,400
13,430

54,050 COVERED SURFACE SQUARE FEET

INTENSITY

can vary widely from bird to bird. The larger the territory, the greater its reach. Its frequencies can change as well: the lower the frequency, the greater the coverage.

Strengthening Ties

Some songbirds develop very complex singing rituals. The duet is perhaps the most striking because it requires both a shared repertoire and good coordination between both birds. In general, the male initiates the song with a repeated introduction; the female then alternates with different phrasing. The phrasing allows for more or less cyclical variations that make it unique. It is believed that this strengthens ties between the pair (as demarcation of territory does) and serves as a stimulus for cooperative behaviors, such as nest building, in which both the male and female may participate.

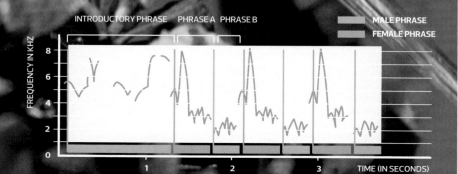

INTRODUCTORY PHRASE PHRASE A PHRASE B

MALE PHRASE
FEMALE PHRASE

FREQUENCY IN KHZ

8
6
4
2

1 2 3 TIME (IN SECONDS)

Nuptial Parade

Finding a mate is not easy for any species. For birds, the exhibition of plumage with bright colors, the presentation of offerings and gifts, and the performance of dances and highly elaborate flight patterns are some of the particular behaviors seen during this period. They are known as nuptial or courtship displays. The male resorts to all these strategic gestures to attract the female's attention and prevent her from paying attention to other males. Some of these rituals are extremely complicated; others are very tender and delicate.

A

When its sexual arousal peaks, the male northern harrier (*Circus cyaneus*) flies in a wavelike pattern to attract the female.

B

During courtship, the male northern harrier pretends to attack the female.

AERIAL EXHIBITIONS

Certain birds, such as goshawks or male northern harriers, court the female in flight. They ascend in the air in broad circles, only to let themselves fall in daring, sharp dives.

MUTUAL DANCES AND COURTSHIPS

Great crested grebes (*Podiceps cristatus*) perform incredible aquatic dances. They bow to each other, dive, and run through the water side by side.

Special Courtship

Avian courtship is a phenomenon that, depending on the species, can take the form of various rituals. Lek rituals are one of the most intriguing forms of courtship. The males gather in a small area, called an arena, where they perform their courtship displays for the females. The females form a circle around the arena and end up mating with the male that has the most striking secondary sexual characteristics. Lek is a system controlled by the dominant male, who ends up mating with most of the females (polygyny). The less experienced males will mate with only a few, or sometimes none, of the females. For some species, lek rituals can be very intricate. At least 85 species perform this special type of courtship ritual, among them manakins, pheasants, cotingas, and hummingbirds. Manakins, for example, stand in line and wait their turn to perform.

DISPLAYING PHYSICAL ATTRIBUTES

To find a partner, birds such as the snowy egret resort to a series of very elaborate signals, such as songs, poses, dances, flight patterns, noisemaking, and displays of their ornamental feathers.

BUILDING BOWERS

Australian bowerbirds build a structure called a bower, which they decorate with pieces of paper and fabric that inevitably attract the female.

GIFTS

Another courtship strategy is the presentation of gifts. Male eagles give females prey, and European bee-eaters offer insects. These offerings are called courtship food.

TIMING

The courtship display is directly related to reproduction cycles. It takes place before copulation, although it can continue to occur thereafter.

Prenuptial
Prenuptial courtship starts with territorial establishment and the search for a partner, which can take place simultaneously.

Postnuptial
With this display, the great crested grebe ensures the continuity of the pairing even after the eggs are laid.

5.9 feet (1.8 m)

IS THE SIZE OF THE TAIL OF THE PEACOCK WHEN IT UNFURLS ITS MORE THAN 200 SHINING FEATHERS AND FORMS A FAN TO ATTRACT THE FEMALE.

Gray Crowned Crane
Balearica regulorum
Two cranes perform a courtship dance consisting of a series of impressive leaps.

Emperor Penguin
Aptenodytes forsteri
A monogamous species. Each recognizes its partner by its voice, and couples will spend their entire lives together.

Monogamy or Polygamy

Monogamy is the most common mating system, in which two birds, one of each sex, participate, leading to the formation of a couple. This couple can endure for a single reproductive season or for life. Polygamy is an alternative pattern, but it is not very common. Polygamy is divided into two classes: polygyny, in which the male mates with several females, and polyandry, in which the female mates with several males (and may even be able to keep them all together in a harem). In either case, one partner has the sole responsibility of caring for the eggs and chicks. There is also an exceptional case within polygamy: promiscuity. In this arrangement, a couple is not formed, and the relationship is limited to copulation.

Home Sweet Home

M ost birds lay their eggs in a nest, where they are incubated by the body heat of an adult sitting on them. To build a nest, the couple normally uses mud mixed with saliva, small stones, branches, and feathers. When the nest is in a visible location, the bird covers it with lichens or loose twigs to hide it from predators. Nest shapes vary according to the bird group: they can take the form of a bowl, a hole in a tree (woodpeckers), or an excavated burrow on a slope of sand or soil. There are even birds that use nests built by other species.●

SOME VARIATIONS

WOVEN NESTS
Weaver birds intertwine grass blades until they form a structure. The entrances are underneath.

BURROWS
Parrots and kingfishers dig their nests in sandy river banks.

SEWN NESTS
The tailorbird sews two large leaves together with grass blades. The nest is inside the leaves.

PLATFORM NESTS
The sparrow hawk gathers a large number of branches and assembles a high, solid base for its eggs.

Types and Locations

Nests are classified according to their shape, material, and location. They vary depending on the amount of warmth the species needs, as well as in terms of the level of protection they offer. The greater the pressure from predators, the higher or better hidden a nest must be. Good examples are isolated nests resembling high platforms; nests in deep depressions in the soil or hidden in tree trunks, which are very safe and provide good insulation; and nests made of clay, which are very hard. The most typical nests resemble a cup and are found at various locations, most often between two or three high, remote branches.

LINING
It is composed of fibers, hairs, feathers, and down. It insulates the eggs from the cold and helps with incubation.

How the Nest is Built

A cup-shaped nest is built at a fork between two or three branches. The bird arranges twigs, grass blades, and small sticks, as if building a platform. The bird then interlaces some of these materials with the tree to give the nest solidity. It then interweaves the materials in a circular pattern. As the nest takes shape, lighter, more adhesive materials—such as mud, spiderwebs, caterpillar silk, and certain plant fibers—are used. Although the outside is rough, the inside is lined with feathers for softness and warmth. Usually if both the male and female participate in the construction, a few hundred trips are enough to complete the nest. In some species, such as weavers, males have to display a nest during courtship; in others (African black eagles, for instance), the same nest is used every year.

THE LITTLE MASKED WEAVER builds solid nests, weaving together leaves and grass blades. Sometimes, the male builds several nests before the female chooses him.

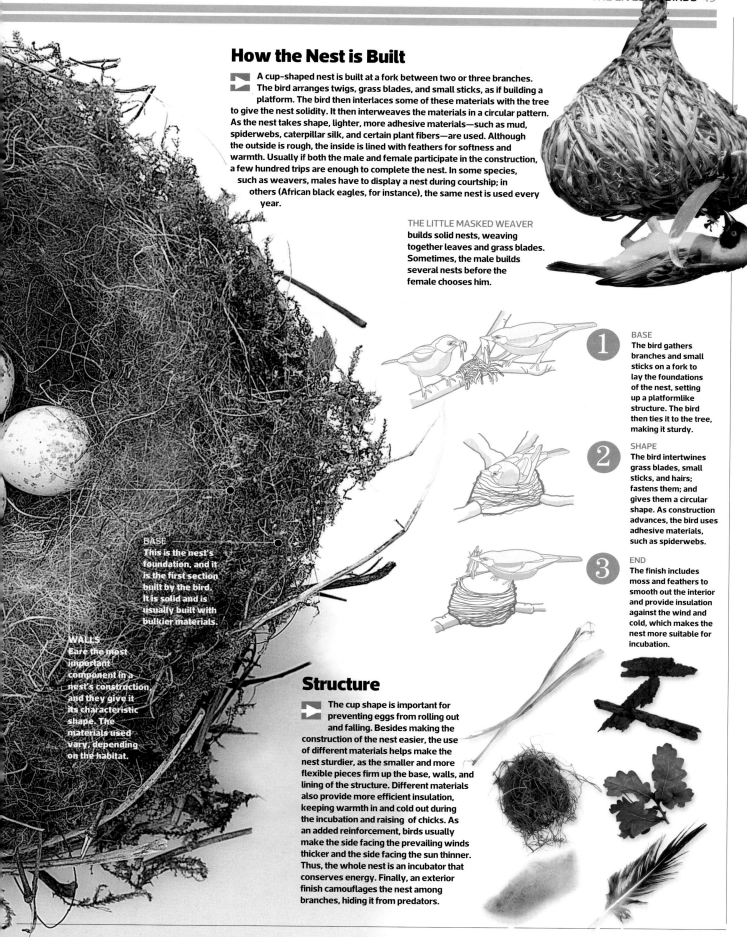

BASE
This is the nest's foundation, and it is the first section built by the bird. It is solid and is usually built with bulkier materials.

WALLS
Walls are the most important component in a nest's construction, and they give it its characteristic shape. The materials used vary, depending on the habitat.

1 BASE
The bird gathers branches and small sticks on a fork to lay the foundations of the nest, setting up a platformlike structure. The bird then ties it to the tree, making it sturdy.

2 SHAPE
The bird intertwines grass blades, small sticks, and hairs; fastens them; and gives them a circular shape. As construction advances, the bird uses adhesive materials, such as spiderwebs.

3 END
The finish includes moss and feathers to smooth out the interior and provide insulation against the wind and cold, which makes the nest more suitable for incubation.

Structure

The cup shape is important for preventing eggs from rolling out and falling. Besides making the construction of the nest easier, the use of different materials helps make the nest sturdier, as the smaller and more flexible pieces firm up the base, walls, and lining of the structure. Different materials also provide more efficient insulation, keeping warmth in and cold out during the incubation and raising of chicks. As an added reinforcement, birds usually make the side facing the prevailing winds thicker and the side facing the sun thinner. Thus, the whole nest is an incubator that conserves energy. Finally, an exterior finish camouflages the nest among branches, hiding it from predators.

First, the Egg

B irds may have inherited their reproductive method from their predecessors, the theropod reptiles. In general, they lay as many eggs as they can care for until the chicks become independent. Highly adapted to the environment, the eggs of the same species have varying shapes and colors. These variations help keep them safe from predators. They also vary greatly in size: the egg of an ostrich is 2,000 times bigger than that of a hummingbird. ●

3 Most birds' organs are formed in the first hours of incubation.

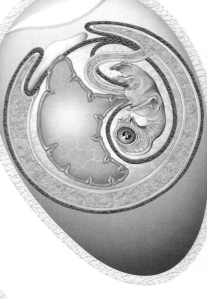

How it Forms

Birds have only one functional ovary, the left one, which grows dramatically during the mating season. The ovule can descend and form what are known as unfertilized eggs (the type used in cooking). If the egg is fertilized, embryonic development begins. The ovule, fertilized or not, descends to the cloaca in a few hours or days. The eggshell begins to be formed at the isthmus, through the secretion of calcium. At first soft, the shell hardens when it comes in contact with the air.

2 As it feeds to grow, the embryo produces waste that is kept in a special sac.

OVULE

1 OVULES
They lie in follicles, arranged like a bunch of grapes.

2 DESCENT
Once fertilized, the ovule travels down the oviduct until it reaches the isthmus.

ISTHMUS

3 SHELL
In the isthmus, the shell membranes form.

5 CLOACA
It expels the egg 24 hours later on average (chicken hens).

4 UTERUS
The egg becomes pigmented, and the shell hardens.

CLOACA

—— WASTE SAC

—— CHORION
protects and contains the embryo and its food.

—— YOLK

—— YOLK SAC

—— ALBUMIN

1

The egg contains an embryo in one side of the yolk. The yolk is held in the middle of the white (albumin) by a protein cord that isolates it from the outside world.

EMBRYO

PROTEIN CORD (CHALAZA)

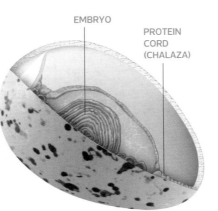

SHAPE
It depends on the pressure exerted by the oviduct walls. The large end emerges first.

Oval: The most frequent	Conical: Prevents falling	Spherical: Reduces the surface area

COLOR AND TEXTURE
Both texture and color help parents locate the egg.

Light Egg	Dark Egg	Speckled Egg

LAYING
A group of eggs laid at one time is called a laying. During the mating season, a sparrow can have several layings. If some eggs are removed, the sparrow can replace them without difficulty.

AIR
SAC

4

The bill and scales of the legs harden toward the end, when the chick is formed and reaches a size similar to the egg. At that point, rotation begins so that the chick will be positioned to break its shell.

SIZE
There is no exact proportion between the size of a bird and its egg.

1 lb
(500 g)
Kiwi Egg

2 oz
(60 g)
Chicken Hen Egg

5

When the chick is ready to break the shell, it is taking up all the space inside the egg. The chick is cramped with its legs against its chest. This enables it to open the shell with small movements and with the help of a hard point at the tip of its bill (called an egg tooth).

YOLK AND WHITE
They decrease in size.

THE SHELL
Formed by a solid layer of calcium carbonate (calcite), it has pores that make it possible for the chick to breathe. Bacteria are kept out by two membranes that cover the egg, one on the inside and the other on the outside.

Pore **Membrane** **Outer and Inner Membranes**

Oxygen

CO_2 and Water Vapor

8%

THE PROPORTION OF AN EGG TAKEN UP BY THE EGGSHELL

ALBUMIN
was consumed.

YOLK
disappears into the body.

Birth in Detail

W hen a chick is about to hatch, it starts to make itself heard from inside the egg. This allows it to communicate with its parents. It then starts to peck at the shell with its tiny egg tooth, which is lost after birth. Next, it turns inside the egg and opens a crack with new perforations, at the same time pushing with its neck and legs until it manages to stick out its head. This job demands a lot of effort and can take 30 to 40 minutes or, in the case of kiwis and albatrosses, even three to four days. In most species, newborn chicks are blind and naked, and they can open their bills only to receive food. ●

INCUBATION

For the embryo to develop, it needs constant temperatures between 99° and 100° F (37–38° C). The parents ensure these temperatures by sitting on the eggs and warming them with their brood patches.

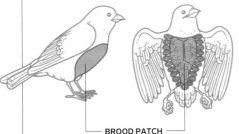

During incubation, some species lose their chest feathers and increase their number of blood vessels in this area. Others pluck out their feathers. Direct contact with the eggs helps keep them warm.

BROOD PATCH

DURATION BY SPECIES

The incubation period varies considerably: between 10 and 80 days, depending on the species.

PIGEON
Females and males incubate. They both develop a brood patch.

18 days

PENGUIN
Both males and females incubate. The emperor male has a special pouch for incubation.

62 days

ALBATROSS
Lacking brood patches, the parents hold the egg between their feet and abdomen.

80 days

Breaking the Shell

 This process may take from a few minutes to three or four days, depending on the species. In general, the parents do not intervene or help their young. When the shell is empty, they throw it out of the nest, to avoid attracting the attention of predators. In species whose young hatch with the feathers already developed, hatching is extremely important. It has been observed that the singing of the chicks stimulates the stragglers and delays those that have gotten ahead; it is important that they all be ready to leave the nest together.

35 minutes

IS THE APPROXIMATE TIME IT TAKES A SPARROW TO COME OUT OF THE EGG.

1

CRACK IN THE EGG
The chick turns inside until its bill targets the egg's midline. It then punctures the air sac. With a few more tries, it pierces the shell. The chick then breathes for the first time.

ASKING FOR HELP
The chick calls for its parents from inside. The reply encourages it to continue the effort.

SEQUENCE OF PECKING
Between each sequence of pecking, the chick must take long breaks.

Adaptations for Hatching

 Getting out of the egg is an intricate operation because the space is tight, and a chick's muscles have little vigor. Birds count on a few adaptations, such as the egg tooth and the hatching muscle, to accomplish the task. The tooth is used for making the first perforation, which allows air into the egg. The muscle exerts the necessary strength, while stimulating the chicken's motor functions to intensify the effort. Both the egg tooth and the hatching muscle disappear shortly after the eggshell is broken.

HATCHING MUSCLE
It exerts pressure against the shell and helps to break it.

EGG TOOTH
A protuberance on the bill that punctures the egg. Its presence depends on the species.

THE CHICK IS BORN
Once outside, the chick, almost featherless, looks for warmth and food from its parents. In the case of some birds that hatch without feathers, not all eggs hatch simultaneously; this benefits the firstborn if food is scarce.

A GREAT EFFORT
Getting out of the shell requires much energy from the chick.

SHELL MEMBRANE

EGGSHELL

GETTING OUT OF THE EGG
Once the shell is open, the chick pushes itself out with its legs and by crawling on its abdomen. For birds that hatch without feathers, this is more difficult, because they are less developed.

THE CRACK EXPANDS
After making a hole in the shell, the chick opens a crack with successive pecks at other points. Air gets in and dries up the membrane, which makes the task easier.

WHAT COMES OUT FIRST?
The head usually comes out first, because the sharp bill helps break the shell. Most birds then get out of the egg by pushing themselves out with their legs. For wading birds and other terrestrial birds, however, the wings usually unfold first.

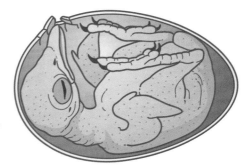

Postnatal Development

Chicks develop at highly variable rates after hatching. Some birds are born with their eyes open and with a thick layer of down feathers. These birds can also feed themselves. That is why they are called precocious, or nidifugous. Ducks, rheas, ostriches, and certain beach birds can walk and swim as soon as they are born. Other species are born naked and develop their feathers later. They need to stay in the nest until they have sufficiently developed, so adult birds must care for them. These birds are called nidicolous. The most helpless chicks are the young of songbirds and hummingbirds, because they need warmth from their parents to grow strong. ●

Nidifugous Young

Nidifugous young are fully developed at the moment of birth. They can move and even leave the nest, hence their name (which means "fleeing the nest"). This adaptation demands more incubation time because the chick is almost fully developed at birth. This is the case with incubator birds *(Megapodius freycinet)*, which begin their independent lives in the outside world as soon as they leave the shell. Ducks follow their parents but find food on their own, whereas chickens follow their parents, who show them where to find food.

EYE
They are born with open eyes.

FEATHERS
The body emerges from the egg covered with damp down. Within three hours, it will become dry and fluffy.

Red-Legged Partridge
Alectoris rufa

MOVEMENT
Within a few hours of hatching, nidifugous birds can run around.

21 days
It is already considered an adult. Its flights are longer. Its diet is composed of 97 percent vegetables; the rest is made up of lichens and insects.

15 days
It starts to perform short flights. It reverses its diet, eating:

66% seeds and flowers. The rest consists of invertebrates.

GROWTH STAGES

30 hours
The chick keeps warm with the down that covers its body. It can walk and begins to be fed by its parents.

7 to 8 days
Growth quickens, and the first covert feathers appear at the tip of the wing. The bird leaves the nest. Its diet consists of:

66% invertebrates. The rest consists of seeds and flowers.

24 hours
IS THE MINIMUM AMOUNT OF TIME THE BLACK-HEADED DUCK NEEDS TO BE READY TO FLY.

SIZE COMPARISON

NIDIFUGOUS
The egg is larger, the chick is born more developed, and the incubation period is longer than that of nidicolous birds.

NIDICOLOUS
They lay small eggs with a brief incubation period, and the young are helpless at birth.

Nidicolous Broods

Most of these chicks are born naked, with closed eyes and with only enough strength to get out of their shells. They stay in the nest. For the first few days, they cannot even regulate their own body temperature; they depend on their parents to stay warm. Within one week, they have a few feathers, but they require constant care and food. They form a numerically important group that includes Passeriformes (songbirds).

FOOD
They need much food to develop. The parents must feed them 24 hours a day.

House Sparrow
Passer domesticus

An adult bird can feed its young up to
400 times a day.

INTERIOR OF THE BILL
Its color is bright to stimulate the parents to regurgitate the food.

Shining Areas

Some species have shiny areas that can even be seen in the dark.

EYES
Nidicolous chicks are born blind. They open their eyes a few days after birth.

FEATHERS
The chicks are born either naked or with down feathers in some areas.

12-15 days
Development is complete, and the covert feathers are ready for flight. All that remains is for the bird to reach adult size.

10 days
Feathers cover their entire body, but they are not yet developed. The chick can stay warm on its own, and it is voracious. Growth is very fast.

8 days
Feathers cover the chick almost completely, except around its eyes. Its legs are well developed, and the sparrow moves around in the nest.

STAGES OF GROWTH

25 hours
It performs a few instinctive movements. It can barely raise its head to ask for food.

4 days
The eyes open. The tips of the first feathers appear. It performs a few movements.

6 days
Some feathers begin to unfold, the nails are formed, and the wings continue to grow with the body. It can stand up.

12-15 days
IS THE ESTIMATED TIME THAT IT TAKES THIS NIDICOLOUS CHICK TO LEAVE THE NEST.

A Diet for Flying

Most birds eat assorted foods that are rich in energy and proteins. Their high level of activity requires that they eat almost constantly. Their sources of food vary and include seeds, fruits, nectar, leaves, insects and other invertebrates, and meat of all kinds (including carrion). Many species eat more than one type of food; some even alternate according to the seasons and migration cycle. This guarantees their survival. However, there are other birds—a minority—that consume only one type of food, for which they have no competition. Because their dependence on this single source of food is greater, though, the risk is higher. Feeding behavior also varies among different species. For example, some eat alone, and others eat in groups. ●

LAMELLAE

TONGUE

From Parents to Children

Flamingos and pigeons feed their young a special "milk" that is produced in the crop and has a nutritional value similar to the milk of mammals. Both males and females produce it as soon as food is ingested so that the chick is not fed regurgitated food.

2. It is given to the young through the bill. Easy to digest and nutritious, it is an excellent food.

A Complex System

Feeding on microorganisms that live in salty water demands a complex filtration system. The flamingo's bill is specially suited to this task. Its tongue and throat pump the water inside the bill as they ascend and descend, bringing water through the hornlike lamellae, which resemble whale baleen, to retain the food passing through them. Their tongues also have a depressed area, where the stones and sediments that come in with the water collect. The whole operation requires that the flamingo submerge its bill upside down. Because of the number of microorganisms they need to consume and the time it takes to filter them, flamingos usually spend many hours in the water. The risks involved in this activity are mitigated by the fact that flamingos do not eat alone, but rather in groups. Occasionally, there are instances of aggression, possibly because of territorial conflicts.

Filtration of Food

1 The flamingo submerges its bill in the briny water to feed on the microorganisms living there.

3 A second filtration occurs inside the bill, as the water is expelled. The lamellae (small plates) catch the microorganisms but let water and other matter pass.

2 The flamingo fills its bill with water by raising its tongue. By doing this, the flamingo performs an initial filtration that keeps out undesired substances.

Cross-Section of the Bill

LOWER MANDIBLE

Tongue

Lamellae

UPPER MANDIBLE

Hooks to Hold the Bill

WATER IN MOTION

Types of Diet

Birds expend a great deal of energy, and their diet must be suited to their high metabolic rates. They eat practically anything, although the diet of some birds is very specific. The same foods are not always available, which causes most birds to adjust their diets throughout the year.

THE HUMMINGBIRD'S TONGUE
Long channeled or tubular tongues suck the nectar and catch insects at the bottom of the corolla of a flower.

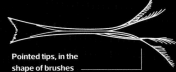

Pointed tips, in the shape of brushes

1.
The flamingo produces milk in its crop only when it is not eating. A protein called prolactin participates in its preparation, just as with mammals.

3.
This milk has high concentrations of the pigment that colors the feathers; that is why the bird's color changes to the characteristic pink while molting in adolescence.

NECTAR
is a solution of sugar and water that flowers produce. It is very high in energy and easy to digest. In order to get it, a bird must have a long, sharp bill. In temperate regions, nectar is plentiful in the spring and summer, whereas in the tropical regions, it is available year round. Hummingbirds and honeycreepers are very fond of this juice.

SEEDS AND GRAINS
The high energy and protein content of seeds make them an ideal food for birds. The problem is that they are seasonal.

MEAT
Hunting and scavenging birds feed on meat. They rarely specialize in one type of prey, but the prey's size determines its selection.

FISH
The abundance of fish throughout the year makes them one of the favorite foods of marine birds. They have a high nutritional value.

LEAVES AND PLANTS
Few birds feed on leaves because they have low energy value. Birds that do have undergone adaptations that permit them to digest cellulose.

FRUIT
In the tropics, this diet is very common because fruits are available throughout the year. In temperate and cold regions, fruit can be found only in the summer. Fruit has a high energy value, and many birds eat it.

INSECTIVORES
Insects are rich in energy and proteins, and they are highly abundant. Thus, many bird species eat them. In cold regions, they can be found only in the summer.

Strategies

Depending on the abundance of resources, the needs of the species, and the strategies for getting food, birds may eat alone or in groups. If food is scarce or widely scattered throughout a region, birds eat alone and defend their territory. On the other hand, if food is abundant, they prefer to eat within the safe confines of the group.

SOLITARY
Usually birds of prey, such as eagles and owls, hunt alone because food is scarce and is randomly distributed. Hunting alone has a drawback in that birds must also watch out for predators, which takes time away from hunting.

TOGETHER
This behavior is typical of ocean birds, such as pelicans and seagulls, and of aquatic birds, such as flamingos. When birds eat in groups, each group member can warn the others about possible dangers, which is beneficial.

Migration Routes

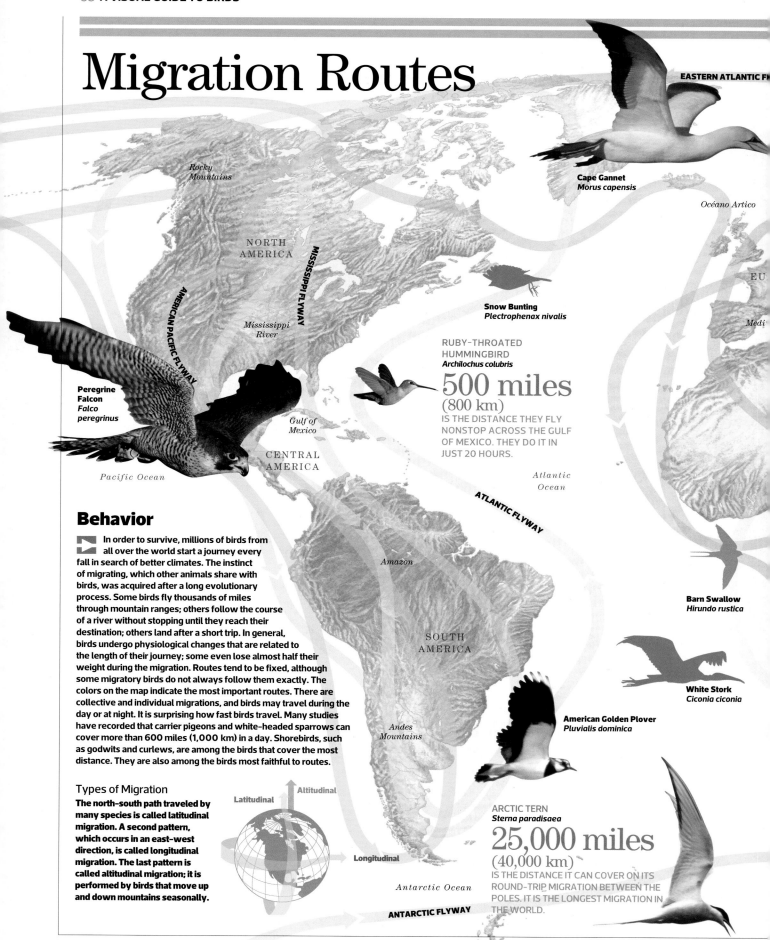

EASTERN ATLANTIC F

Cape Gannet
Morus capensis

Océano Ártico

EU

Medi

Snow Bunting
Plectrophenax nivalis

RUBY-THROATED HUMMINGBIRD
Archilochus colubris

500 miles
(800 km)
IS THE DISTANCE THEY FLY NONSTOP ACROSS THE GULF OF MEXICO. THEY DO IT IN JUST 20 HOURS.

Peregrine Falcon
Falco peregrinus

Rocky Mountains

NORTH AMERICA

MISSISSIPPI FLYWAY

Mississippi River

AMERICAN PACIFIC FLYWAY

Gulf of Mexico

CENTRAL AMERICA

Pacific Ocean

Atlantic Ocean

ATLANTIC FLYWAY

Amazon

Andes Mountains

SOUTH AMERICA

Barn Swallow
Hirundo rustica

White Stork
Ciconia ciconia

American Golden Plover
Pluvialis dominica

Behavior

In order to survive, millions of birds from all over the world start a journey every fall in search of better climates. The instinct of migrating, which other animals share with birds, was acquired after a long evolutionary process. Some birds fly thousands of miles through mountain ranges; others follow the course of a river without stopping until they reach their destination; others land after a short trip. In general, birds undergo physiological changes that are related to the length of their journey; some even lose almost half their weight during the migration. Routes tend to be fixed, although some migratory birds do not always follow them exactly. The colors on the map indicate the most important routes. There are collective and individual migrations, and birds may travel during the day or at night. It is surprising how fast birds travel. Many studies have recorded that carrier pigeons and white-headed sparrows can cover more than 600 miles (1,000 km) in a day. Shorebirds, such as godwits and curlews, are among the birds that cover the most distance. They are also among the birds most faithful to routes.

Types of Migration

The north-south path traveled by many species is called latitudinal migration. A second pattern, which occurs in an east-west direction, is called longitudinal migration. The last pattern is called altitudinal migration; it is performed by birds that move up and down mountains seasonally.

Altitudinal

Latitudinal

Longitudinal

Antarctic Ocean

ANTARCTIC FLYWAY

ARCTIC TERN
Sterna paradisaea

25,000 miles
(40,000 km)
IS THE DISTANCE IT CAN COVER ON ITS ROUND-TRIP MIGRATION BETWEEN THE POLES. IT IS THE LONGEST MIGRATION IN THE WORLD.

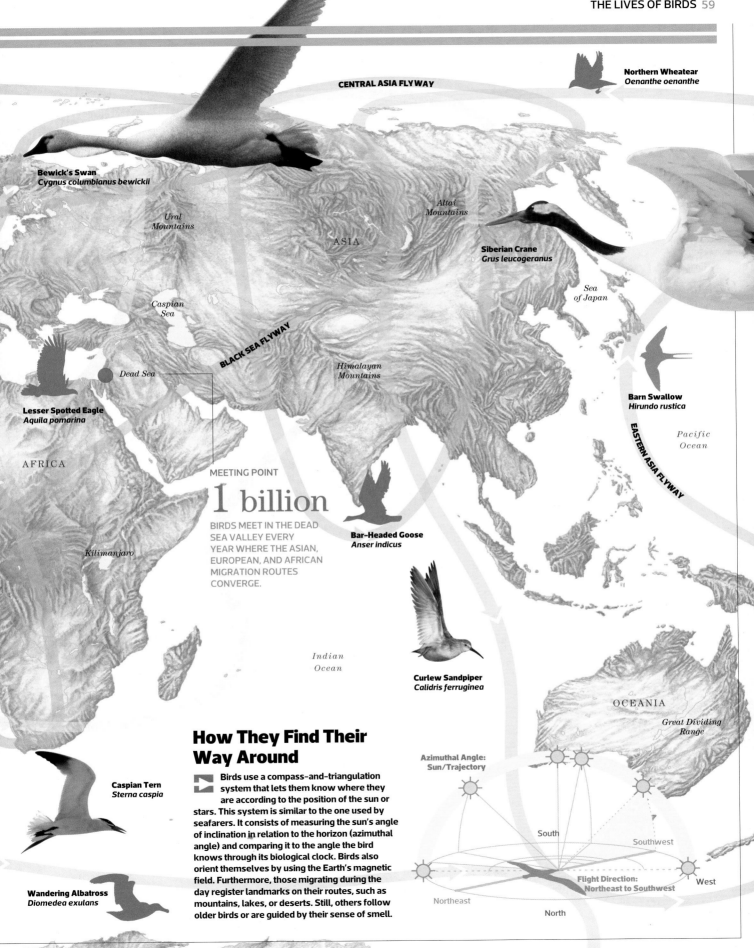

Northern Wheatear
Oenanthe oenanthe

CENTRAL ASIA FLYWAY

Bewick's Swan
Cygnus columbianus bewickii

Ural Mountains

Altai Mountains

ASIA

Siberian Crane
Grus leucogeranus

Caspian Sea

Sea of Japan

BLACK SEA FLYWAY

Himalayan Mountains

Barn Swallow
Hirundo rustica

Dead Sea

Lesser Spotted Eagle
Aquila pomarina

Pacific Ocean

AFRICA

EASTERN ASIA FLYWAY

MEETING POINT

1 billion

BIRDS MEET IN THE DEAD SEA VALLEY EVERY YEAR WHERE THE ASIAN, EUROPEAN, AND AFRICAN MIGRATION ROUTES CONVERGE.

Bar-Headed Goose
Anser indicus

Kilimanjaro

Curlew Sandpiper
Calidris ferruginea

Indian Ocean

OCEANIA

Great Dividing Range

How They Find Their Way Around

Birds use a compass-and-triangulation system that lets them know where they are according to the position of the sun or stars. This system is similar to the one used by seafarers. It consists of measuring the sun's angle of inclination in relation to the horizon (azimuthal angle) and comparing it to the angle the bird knows through its biological clock. Birds also orient themselves by using the Earth's magnetic field. Furthermore, those migrating during the day register landmarks on their routes, such as mountains, lakes, or deserts. Still, others follow older birds or are guided by their sense of smell.

Azimuthal Angle: Sun/Trajectory

South

Southwest

Caspian Tern
Sterna caspia

West

Flight Direction: Northeast to Southwest

Northeast

Wandering Albatross
Diomedea exulans

North

Defense Strategies

Birds have many predators, including cats, snakes, crocodiles, and other birds. To defend themselves against these predators, birds use various strategies, the most common of which is camouflage. Some birds blend in with their surroundings and thus go unnoticed by their enemies. Chaparrel birds, whose plumage colors and patterns make them difficult to discern when they are on the ground, use this strategy. Other birds take flight in the face of a threat. There are also those that keep still in the presence of unknown animals, feigning death, whereas others face an enemy and fight. It is not uncommon to see magpies, thrushes, and other birds chasing away strangers that get close to their nests.

Individual Strategies

Among solitary birds, it is common to flee quickly if a stranger is present. Not all solitary birds react this way, though; some have developed specific techniques to defend themselves.

ESCAPE
In the presence of terrestrial predators, a bird's first reaction is to take flight. If the bird cannot fly, it looks for shelter or a hiding place.

EXPANSION
Owls spread out their wings to look bigger than they really are.

DISTRACTION
Little bustards shoot their excrement in the face of birds that prey on them. This distracts the predator and makes it possible to escape.

CAMOUFLAGE
is very common and is one of the most efficient defensive strategies. Many birds develop plumage to imitate the dominant colors and shapes of the environment where they live. When they notice the presence of a potential enemy, they stay motionless to avoid calling attention to themselves. There are a few notable cases, such as that of the tawny frogmouth (*Podargus strigoides*), pictured above. Many partridges and terrestrial birds are experts at the art of blending in with the landscape; the rock ptarmigan, for example, has white plumage in the winter that becomes terra-cotta in the summer.

Defense of the Brood

Hatching and youth are times of critical vulnerability for birds. During these phases, they are forced to keep still because they are easy prey. For this reason, parents permanently watch over their nests, even attacking strangers if they get too close.

FEIGNING INJURY
A very widespread behavior is to pretend to be wounded or sick. This allows a bird to avoid being chosen as prey. This behavior is common among warblers, partridges, and pigeons.

ATTACK
In other situations, birds adopt openly aggressive behaviors in the presence of intruders or predators. Magpies can even hound and chase away eagles if the latter threaten their brood. Such active defenses are more common among birds of prey.

PROTECTION
When a parent detects danger, it gets close to its young and covers them so that they are not alone. This behavior is common among tropical birds (tropical seabirds). Several species of curlews and sandpipers place their young between their legs, whereas grebes carry their chicks on their backs when swimming.

Collective Strategies

Birds that have group behaviors usually develop group strategies to protect themselves against predators. Being numerous is a guarantee that the species will go on. They also adopt other tactics as a group.

COLONIES
A great number of birds can defend themselves better from predators when in groups. For that reason they even form colonies with other bird species when raising their young.

FLOCK
In the presence of predators, birds form flocks that fly in a synchronized manner, which makes it hard for the predators to focus on any one individual.

ATTACKS AND COLLECTIVE AID
Many birds that live in groups have developed several hounding behaviors in the presence of potential enemies. They perform them to help an individual that is in danger or is unable to flee.

WARNING
They emit callings that warn the whole colony. The great majority of species have a specific and characteristic cry that is usually simple, brief, and very audible.
They often emit these warnings while adopting postures (such as stretching the neck or shaking the wings) that alone are enough to warn other individuals of the intruder's presence.

1 **2** **3**

TO DEFEND ITSELF from the falcon's attack, a flock of starlings squeezes together in a dense formation. If they are near a tree, they do not hesitate to hide in it.

Diversity and Distribution

The environment in which an organism usually lives is called its habitat. In their habitats, birds find food, the best places to build nests, and escape routes in case of danger. An almost universal pattern of distribution shows that more species live in the tropics than elsewhere. With evolution, birds with a common origin have diversified

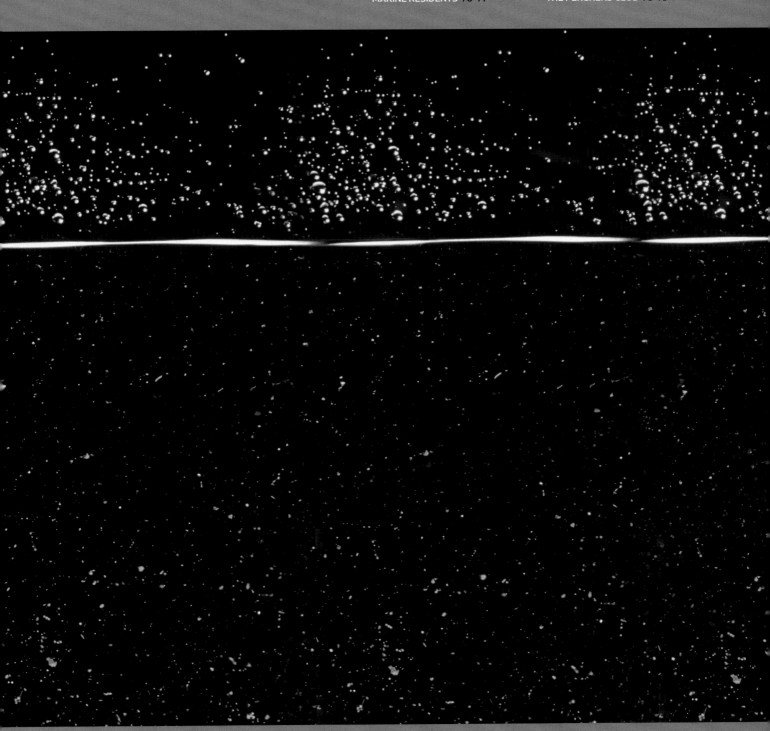

DUCK (Anatidae family)
A natural-born fisher, ducks feed on small snails and aquatic insect larvae.

as they have begun to occupy different environments. This phenomenon is called adaptive radiation. We find ocean birds, which have undergone many changes in order to live near the sea, as well as birds that live in freshwater environments, in forests, and so on. Each type has acquired special physical traits and behaviors as a result of the adaptive process. ●

One Bird, One Name

To learn more about different birds, we give each species a name. Ancient peoples grouped birds according to practical traits and mystical beliefs. They used birds as food or considered them to be bad omens or symbols of good luck. The people who developed scientific thought created a classification system that took into consideration the external form as well as the behavior of these vertebrates; hence, the denominations predator, wading bird, and songbird were developed, among others. The most recent system of classification, which is based on genetic and evolutionary criteria, has generated a hierarchical organization of names that is constantly being updated. ●

HOATZIN
Opisthocomus hoazin
is a tropical bird species that inhabits the Amazon. The presence of talons on the chicks' heels links them to their earliest ancestors, including *Archaeopteryx*.

What is a Classification?

Since the early Renaissance in the 16th century, scientific classifications assigned compound names to birds, as well as to other living creatures. The first part stands for a genus and the second for a specific name. Thus, the rock (domestic) pigeon is called *Columba livia* in scientific terms. The discovery of new species in different parts of the world widened the array of birds so that compound names were no longer enough. The level of family was established to group genera of birds that share similar traits. In turn, bird families that share common traits were grouped into orders. These were then combined into a category called class. Classes include all current and extinct birds. Birds share a higher category in the hierarchy Ωthe phylumΩ with fish, amphibians, reptiles, mammals, and vertebrates in general.

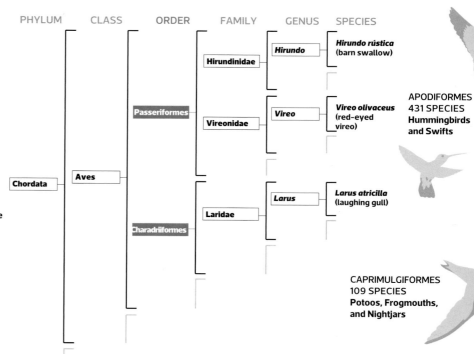

PHYLUM	CLASS	ORDER	FAMILY	GENUS	SPECIES
			Hirundinidae	*Hirundo*	*Hirundo rústica* (barn swallow)
		Passeriformes	Vireonidae	*Vireo*	*Vireo olivaceus* (red-eyed vireo)
Chordata	Aves				
		Charadriiformes	Laridae	*Larus*	*Larus atricilla* (laughing gull)

APODIFORMES
431 SPECIES
Hummingbirds and Swifts

CAPRIMULGIFORMES
109 SPECIES
Potoos, Frogmouths, and Nightjars

SPHENISCIFORMES
18 SPECIES
Penguins

GAVIIFORMES
5 SPECIES
Loons (diving birds)

PROCELLARIIFORMES
110 SPECIES
Albatrosses, Petrels, and Fulmars

PODICIPEDIFORMES
21 SPECIES
Grebes

ANSERIFORMES
150 SPECIES
Ducks, Geese, and Swans

PELECANIFORMES
62 SPECIES
Pelicans, Boobies, and Cormorants

Diversity and the Environment

Living birds are distributed among a wide variety of habitats. They can be found in aquatic (freshwater or marine) and aero-terrestrial environments. Marine birds live on cliffs, on islands, or in mangrove swamps. They are excellent fishers, and they use seashores or crannies between rocks as refuges for nesting. In freshwater bodies, such as rivers and streams, ducks feed on plants and surface microorganisms. Muddy shores are rich in insects and mollusks, which are the favorite dishes of ibis. Herons, storks, and egrets spear fish with their sharp bills as they wade in water with their long legs without getting wet. Forests, jungles, mountain ranges, and wide plains form most of the world's aero-terrestrial environments. In jungles and forests, predatory birds hunt their prey, while trogons and parrots gorge on insects and fruit. Rocky peaks are the refuge of condors, which fly for hours in search of the remains of dead animals. Ostriches run over prairies and savannas.

FALCONIFORMES
295 SPECIES
Condors, Buzzards, Eagles, Vultures, and Falcons

COLIIFORMES
6 SPECIES
Mousebirds

PSITTACIFORMES
360 SPECIES
Parrots, Parakeets, Lories, Cockatoos, and Macaws

CORACIIFORMES
204 SPECIES
Common Kingfishers and Bee-Eaters

PICIFORMES
382 SPECIES
Woodpeckers, Toucans, and Puffbirds

CUCULIFORMES
160 SPECIES
Cuckoos, Turacos, and Hoatzins

COLUMBIFORMES
317 SPECIES
Pigeons and Doves

PASSERIFORMES
5,400 SPECIES
Perching Birds and Songbirds

CHARADRIIFORMES
350 SPECIES
Seagulls, Lapwings, and Plovers

UPUPIFORMES
1 SPECIES
Hoopoe

STRIGIFORMES
174 SPECIES
Owls

TROGONIFORMES
39 SPECIES
Trogons and Quetzals

CICONIIFORMES
120 SPECIES
Herons, Storks, Ibises, and Egrets

GRUIFORMES
190 SPECIES
Moorhens, Cranes, and Coots

STRUTHIONIFORMES
1 SPECIES
Ostrich

PHOENICOPTERIFORMES
1 SPECIES
Flamingos

GALLIFORMES
274 SPECIES
Chickens, Turkeys, Quails, Pheasants, and Partridges

TINAMIFORMES
47 SPECIES
Tinamous

CASUARIIFORMES
4 SPECIES
Cassowaries and Emus

APTERYGIFORMES
4 SPECIES
Kiwis

RHEIFORMES
2 SPECIES
Rheas

Where They Live

With their mobility, birds have conquered all areas of the Earth. Despite this characteristic, there are few cosmopolitan species—that is, most birds have specific habitats determined by climate and geographic features. Count de Buffon in the 18th century was the first person to notice that living beings are not distributed homogeneously. By analyzing how animals were dispersed on the planet, he realized that different places had different types of fauna. After the work of naturalist Charles Darwin and ornithologist Philip Sclater, it became clear that organisms are situated in specific biogeographic regions. ●

NORTH AMERICA

Atlantic Ocean

Pacific Ocean

CENTRAL AMERICA

SOUTH AMERICA

PUFFIN
Fratercula artica

Nearctic

732 Species
62 Families

7 %

CHARACTERISTICS

Climatic barrier of cold weather and oceanic isolation

Most migrating species

Many insectivorous and aquatic birds

Affinity with Palearctic

Endemic Avifauna: **loons and puffins**

Oceania

187 Species
15 Families

2 %

CHARACTERISTICS

Large area and number of climates

Gliders, divers, and swimmers

Abundance of fish-eating species

Many cosmopolitan species

Endemic Avifauna: **albatrosses, sheathbills, petrels, penguins, and seagulls**

Adaptations According to the Environment

Birds are found in all habitats of the world, although most live in tropical regions. Their ability to adapt, however, is remarkable. From jungles to deserts, from mountains to coasts, and even on the sea, birds have succeeded in acclimating themselves. They have undergone a highly varied array of changes in form and behavior. Emperor penguins not only nest in Antarctica but they also incubate their eggs between their feet for 62 to 66 days. The male Lichtenstein's sandgrouse has developed a sponge of feathers to bring water to its chicks, and hummingbirds have special wings that enable them to make all sorts of maneuvers.

Neotropic

3,370 Species
86 Families

32 %

CHARACTERISTICS

Long-lasting geographic isolation

Many primitive species

Great numbers of frugivores

Endemic Avifauna: **rheas, tinamous, oilbirds, hoatzins, cotingas, and stripe-backed antbirds**

This region undoubtedly has the greatest diversity of birds. The variety in the South American tropics, the most important tropical zone in the world, is one and a half times greater than that of tropical Africa. With more than 1,700 species, Colombia, Brazil, and Peru are the countries with the greatest diversity of avifauna. Even Ecuador, a much smaller country, has more than 1,500 species.

HOATZIN
Opisthocomus hoazin

Biodiversity in the World

The most diverse regions in terms of bird populations are the tropics because of the favorable conditions of abundant food and warm climate found in them. Temperate regions, however, with their seasons, are destinations for migrating birds from tropical and polar regions. Cold regions, on the other hand, have little diversity but are rich in population density. The rule is that diversity of life-forms happens in places where the environment requires less severe adaptations.

NUMBER OF SPECIES
- up to 200
- 200 – 400
- 400 – 600
- 600 – 800
- 800 – 1000
- 1000 – 1200
- 1200 – 1400
- 1400 – 1600
- 1600 – 1800

ASIA

Palearctic

937 Species
73 families

9 %

CHARACTERISTICS

Climatic barrier of cold weather and oceanic isolation

Low diversity of species

Most are migratory species

Many insectivorous and aquatic birds

Endemic Avifauna: **wood grouse, waxwings, flycatchers, cranes**

EUROPA

AFRICA

Because of similar climatic conditions, many authors merge the Palearctic and Neoarctic regions, calling the combined region Holarctica.

COUNTRIES WITH THE MOST SPECIES

More than 1,500

Colombia
Brazil
Peru
Ecuador
Indonesia

More than 1,000

Bolivia
Venezuela
China
India
Mexico
Democratic Republic
of the Congo
Tanzania
Kenya
Argentina

Afrotropic

1,950 Species
73 families

19 %

CHARACTERISTICS

Maritime and desert isolation

Great number of Passeriformes

Many flightless birds

Endemic Avifauna: **ostriches, turacos, cuckoos**

Indian Ocean

Pacific Ocean

Indomalaya

1,700 Species
66 families

16 %

CHARACTERISTICS

Affinities with the Afrotropical zone

Tropical birds

Many frugivores

Endemic Avifauna: **ioras, pittas, swifts**

OCEANIA

Australasia

1,590 Species
64 families

15 %

CHARACTERISTICS

Long isolation

Many flightless and primitive birds

Endemic Avifauna: **emus, kiwis, cockatoos, birds of paradise**

RUBY-THROATED HUMMINGBIRD
Archilochus colubris

OSTRICH
Struthio camelus

No Flying Allowed

A few birds have lost their ability to fly. Their main characteristic is wing loss or reduction, although for some a remarkable size may be the cause of their inability to fly. Such birds weigh more than 39 pounds (18 kg). This is the case with runners (ostriches, cassowaries, emus, rheas, kiwis), extremely fast birds that live in remote areas of New Zealand, and swimmers, such as penguins, that have developed extraordinary aquatic abilities. ●

AFRICAN OSTRICH
A single species inhabits eastern and southern Africa. Adults reach a height of 9 feet (2.75 m) and a weight of 330 pounds (150 kg).

Super Swimmers

Penguins' bodies are covered with three layers of small, overlapping feathers. A penguin has small limbs and a hydrodynamic shape that helps it swim with agility and speed. Dense, waterproof plumage and a layer of fat insulate the bird from the low temperatures of the regions where it lives. Since its bones are rigid and compact, it is able to submerge itself easily. This adaptation distinguishes it from flying birds, whose bones are light and hollow.

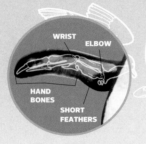

WRIST
ELBOW
HAND BONES
SHORT FEATHERS

FLIPPERS
The short, compact wings look like flippers. They are essential to the penguin's underwater movements.

Rockhopper Penguin
Eudyptes crestatus

SMALL HEAD
LONG NECK
ATROPHIED WINGS
PELVIS

PENGUIN HEADING TO THE WATER

FLAT STERNUM
ROBUST BONE

Runner's Chest
The keel-shaped sternum of flying and swimming birds offers a larger surface for attachment of the pectoral muscles. The flat sternum of running birds has a smaller surface and, consequently, less mobility.

KEEL-SHAPED STERNUM

HUNTING
The wings work like flippers. The foot—with four joined toes pointing backward—and the tail steer the direction of the dive.

BREATHING
When looking for food, penguins need to leave the water and take a breath between plunges.

RELAXING
When resting in the water, they move slowly. They float on the surface with their heads up and balance their bodies with their wings and feet.

The Ratites

Running birds belong to the group of the ratites (*rata* – raft, an allusion to the flat sternum). The front limbs either are atrophied or have functions unrelated to flying. The hind limbs have very strong muscles as well as sturdy, vigorous bones. Another difference is found in the sternum. It is a flat bone without a keel, which flying and swimming birds possess. Wild ratites can be found only in the Southern Hemisphere. The Tinamidae, native to Central and South America, belong to this group (partridges).

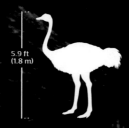

5.9 ft (1.8 m)

STRUTHIONIFORMES
The ostrich is the only species in this group. It uses its wings for balance when running fast. It has only two toes on each foot. The adult male can weigh up to 330 pounds (150 kg).

3.9 ft (1.2 m)

RHEIFORMES
Rhea are common in South American countries, such as Argentina. They look like ostriches but are smaller. Their three-toed feet allow them to chase prey. Their long necks and excellent eyesight make them skillful hunters.

4.6 ft (1.4 m)

CASUARIIFORMES
Agile runners and swimmers. The colors on their necks and heads are distinctive. A bony hoof protects them from vegetation when they run. They have long, sharp talons on their feet.

1.3 ft (0.4 m)

APTERYGIFORMES
Kiwis. These birds have four toes on each foot, and their feathers look like fur because they do not have barbules. They normally use their keen sense of smell to find insects at night. They lay only one large egg.

ASIA

OCEANIA

New Zealand

2 ft (0.6 m)

GREATER DIVERSITY
In many cases, running birds can be found in many parts of the world because of human intervention. The area where flightless birds have diversified the most is Oceania, due to continental isolation.

Running and Kicking

Ostriches usually run to escape from predators or to hunt small lizards and rodents. In both cases, because of their strong legs, they are able to reach a speed of 45 miles per hour (72 km/h) and to maintain it for 20 minutes. When running is not enough to protect the bird, kicking is a valid recourse that discourages the attacker. In courtship displays, forceful stamping is also used to win over females.

18
VERTEBRAE
THE NUMBER AN OSTRICH HAS IN ITS NECK

ON TWO TOES
With just two toes, the contact surface between the foot and the ground is relatively small. This is an advantage when moving on land.

PHALANGES

CLAW

TARSUS METATARSUS

PHALANGEAL CUSHION

TOE

PLANTAR CUSHION

Other Walkers

More than 260 species belong to the order Galliformes, which includes chickens, turkeys, and pheasants. The birds in this group have keels, and they perform abrupt and fast flights, but only in extreme situations. Their feet are suitable for walking, running, and scratching the ground. This group includes the birds that human beings use the most. In general, males are in charge of incubating and raising the young.

FLYING WITH LITTLE GRACE

1 Taking a run and jump

2 Clumsy and flapping fast

3 Emergency landing

Marine Residents

O f the more than 10,000 bird species inhabiting the Earth, only about 300 have managed to adapt to marine life. To survive at sea, they have undergone multiple adaptations. For instance, marine birds have a more efficient excretory system than that of other species, including a specific gland that helps them eliminate excess salt. Most marine birds live on the coasts and have mixed behaviors; others are more aquatic than aerial. A few—such as albatrosses, petrels, and shearwaters—can fly for months at a time, landing only to raise their chicks. They are called pelagic birds.

Adaptations

Marine birds are well prepared to live on water, especially those that fish out at sea. The tips of their bills are hook-shaped, and their feet have webbed membranes between the toes. They also have an admirable ability to float. The saline water is not a problem; these birds can even drink it. In some pelagic birds, sense of smell plays an important role in enabling them to detect the oil of the fish in the water to find schools of fish. They also use their sense of smell to find their nests in colonies.

CORMORANT BILL

Fourth Toe

Membrane

Toe

TOTIPALMATE FEET
A characteristic of many marine birds. The posterior toe (hallux) is joined to the other toes by a membrane. It creates more surface area, and therefore more push, as the bird swims. Birds with this kind of foot walk clumsily.

148 feet (45 m)

IS THE MAXIMUM DEPTH THEY REACH. COMMON LOONS—BIRDS INDIGENOUS TO NORTH AMERICA THAT SPEND THE WINTER AT SEA—HAVE BEEN RECORDED TO REACH THIS DEPTH. ALMOST UNABLE TO WALK, COMMON LOONS ARE EXCELLENT SWIMMERS AND DIVERS. THEY NEST AT INLAND LAKES DURING THE SUMMER.

COMMON LOON
Gavia immer

VARIOUS MARINE BIRDS

HOOK-SHAPED TIP
Prevents the fish from sliding and falling away, once caught

IMPERIAL SHAG
Phalocrocorax atriceps
This great coastal diver has solid bones and strong swimming feet. It does not oil its plumage so that it can better submerge.

BROWN PELICAN
Pelecanus occidentalis
It stays on the shore. It uses its crop as a fishing net while it swims.

HERRING GULL
Larus argentatus
A voracious fisher and great glider. There are many species, some truly cosmopolitan.

CAPE GANNET
Morus capensis
Skillful spearfishers. They live in colonies in Africa. To help cool themselves, they have a strip of naked skin on their throats.

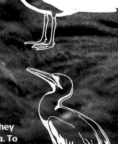

TUBULAR NOSTRILS
Albatrosses have one on each side of their bills. On petrels and shearwaters, the tubular nostrils have merged on top of the bill, forming a single nasal tube.

BILL
It is composed of several hard plates.

Salt Gland

Living in the ocean requires a few adaptations. The most notable one is the salt gland, which eliminates excess salt from the bloodstream. This way, marine birds can even drink salt water without suffering dehydration, as would be the case with humans. This gland is very efficient: it has been observed that 20 to 30 minutes after drinking a saline solution with concentrations similar to that of the ocean (4 percent), birds eliminate another solution (through the nostrils) with 5 percent salt, in the shape of water drops.

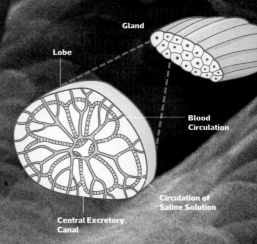

Gland

Lobe

Blood Circulation

Central Excretory Canal

Circulation of Saline Solution

Fishing Methods

Many marine birds fish by diving into the sea. This way, they can access fish that swim below the surface. In order to reach deeper levels in the water, they fly up several feet, spy a school, fold their wings, and plunge with their necks stretched forward. Thanks to the buoyancy of their feathers, they are back on the surface moments later.

DIVE FISHING

1. The bird dives to gain speed.

2. It folds its wings and stretches out its neck to immerse itself in the water and reach the school of fish.

3. The bird immerses its body as much as possible to catch the fish; its feathers cause it to float back up.

Freshwater Birds

This group includes birds that vary greatly—from common kingfishers to ducks to storks—and covers a wide spectrum. Freshwater birds live in rivers, lakes, and ponds for part of the year and are perfectly adapted to aquatic life. Some are excellent swimmers, whereas others are great divers. An important group wades in watercourses with long legs as they fish. Freshwater birds have a varied diet and are mostly omnivorous. ●

Ducks and Distant Cousins

The order Anseriformes includes birds that are very familiar to humans: ducks, geese, and swans, for example. They have short, webbed feet and wide, flat bills lined with lamellae (false teeth) that enable them to filter their food, catch fish, and scrape the beds of rivers and ponds. Most are omnivorous and aquatic (either staying on the surface or diving), although some species spend more time on land. They are widely distributed, and the plumage of males becomes very colorful during the courtship season.

10 to 13 inches (26–33 cm)
Muscovy Duck
Cairina moschata

28 to 34 inches (70–85 cm)
Black-Necked Swan
Cygnus melancoryphus

26 to 34 inches (66–86 cm)
White-Fronted Goose
Anser albifrons

Fulvous Whistling Duck
Dendrocygna bicolor

HOW THEY USE THEIR FEET TO SWIM
A duck moves its feet in two ways. To advance, it spreads out its toes and uses its webbed feet to row. It closes the toes to bring the foot forward again. If the bird wants to turn, only one foot pushes to the side.

Folded Web

Unfolded Web

A DUCK'S DIET

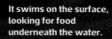
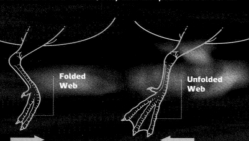

1 It swims on the surface, looking for food underneath the water.

2 It sticks its head into the water, abruptly pushes back its feet and turns its neck downward.

3 It floats face-down and pokes the bottom with its bill.

ORIFICES
Open and oval

LAMELLAE
Around the inside
edges of the bill

Divers and Other Fishers

Diving birds belong to the family Podicipediformes. They feed on small fish and aquatic insects. They are very clumsy on the ground. In the Coraciiformes order, common kingfishers and other similar birds find their prey by closely watching the water. When one of these birds notices a small fish, it spears it, catching it with its bill. In the order Charadriiformes, curlews wander around the edges of ponds in search of food. Their long legs keep their bodies out of the water. They are not swimmers.

DUCK BILLS
are flat, wide, and slightly depressed toward the middle. In general, their shape does not vary, but there are species with tiny bills (the mandarin duck, for example).

12 to 16 in (30–40 cm)

16 in (40 cm)

GREBE
Podiceps sp.

STONE CURLEW
Burhinus oedicnemus

7 in (18 cm)

COMMON KINGFISHER
(also known as European Kingfisher)
Alcedo attlis

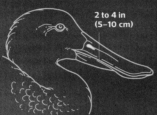

2 to 4 in (5–10 cm)

1 in (2.7 cm)

THE BILL OF AN IBIS
is long and thin, ideal to stick in the mud to look for food.

Shovel-Shaped Bill:
Typical of many ducks. The size varies.

Mandarin Duck Bill:
One of the smallest-billed species.

Wading Birds

These birds belong to an artificial order since, from a genetic perspective, the species are not related. They are grouped together because adaptation to the same habitat has caused them to develop similar shapes: long bills and necks to perform skillful movements and thin legs designed to wade across the water as they fish. Herons form a special group because they are cosmopolitan and because they have powder down feathers. Ibis and storks also have a wide distribution (area in which they occur). Birds that have spoon- and hammer-shaped bills are found primarily in Africa.

White Ibis
Edocimus albus

IBIS (*Ibis* sp.): Some filtrate, and others fish.

STORK (*Ciconia* sp.): It fishes with its long bill.

SHOEBILL (*Balae-niceps rex*): It eats among floating sedges.

HERON (*Egretta* sp.): It fishes with its sharp bill.

COMMON SPOONBILL (*Platalea leucorodia*): It eats several types of aquatic animals.

HAMMERKOP (*Scopus umbretta*): It fishes and hunts small animals.

THE LEGS OF AN IBIS
keep the bird above the water but close enough to fish. Ibis also stir up the beds of lakes and ponds.

Armed to Hunt

Birds of prey are hunters and carnivorous by nature. They are perfectly equipped to eat living animals. Their eyesight is three times sharper than that of human beings; their ears are designed to determine the precise status of their prey; they have strong, sharp talons; and they can kill a small mammal with the pressure of their talons alone. Their hook-shaped bills can kill prey by tearing its neck with a single peck. Eagles, falcons, vultures, and owls are examples of birds of prey. Birds of prey can be diurnal or nocturnal, and they are always on the lookout.

Diurnal and Nocturnal

Eagles, falcons, and vultures are diurnal birds of prey, whereas owls are nocturnal—that is, they are active during the night. These two groups are not closely related. These birds' main prey includes small mammals, reptiles, and insects. Once they locate the victim, they glide toward it. Nocturnal birds of prey are specially adapted: their eyesight is highly developed, their eyes are oriented forward, and their hearing is sharp. The feathers on their wings are arranged in such a way that they make no noise when the bird is flying. In order to protect themselves while sleeping during the day, they have dull plumage, which helps them blend in with their surroundings.

EURASIAN EAGLE OWL
Bubo bubo
Its ears are asymmetrical and can determine the location of prey with great precision.

BALD EAGLE
Haliaeetus leucocephalus
It has a visual field of 220 degrees and a bifocal vision of 50 degrees.

Bills

The bills of birds of prey are hook-shaped. Some birds of prey have a tooth that works like a knife, allowing them to kill their prey, tear its skin and muscle tissues, and get to the food easily. The structure and shape of the bills of birds of prey changes depending on the species. Scavengers (for example, vultures and condors) have weaker bills because the tissues of animals in decomposition are softer. Other species, such as falcons, catch prey with their talons and use their bills to finish it off with a violent stab to the neck, breaking its spine.

CERE
Fleshy formation, somewhat thick and soft

TIP
Where the tooth is located

NOSTRIL
Olfactory canals

Zone-Tailed Hawk
Buteo albonotatus

BALD EAGLE
Its hook-shaped bill is common to many birds of prey.

SPARROW HAWK
Its thin bill enables it to take snails out of their shells.

FALCON
It can break the spine of its prey with its upper bill.

GOSHAWK
Its strong bill can catch prey as large as hares.

OWL PELLETS
Owls produce pellets. They swallow their prey whole and regurgitate the indigestible substances. The study of pellets makes it possible to determine the fauna of small areas with great precision.

OW THE VULTURE HUNTS

1
Vultures feed mainly on carrion, although they are able to attack a living animal if it is vulnerable and the situation presents itself.

2
Thanks to their ability to glide on thermals, vultures can find carcasses on which to feed without wasting energy.

3
Once they find food, they must analyze the territory to know if they will be able to take flight again soon.

DIMENSIONS
The wings of birds of prey are adapted to suit their flying requirements. They can measure up to 10 feet (3 m).

Condors 3 to 9.5 ft (0.95–2.9 m)

Eagles 4.5 to 8 ft (1.35–2.45 m)

Buzzards 4 to 5 ft (1.2–1.5 m)

Kites 2.6 to 6.4 ft (0.8–1.95 m)

Red-Backed Hawk
3.4 to 4.4 ft (1.05–1.35 m)

Falcons 2.2 to 4.1 ft (0.67–1.25 m)

5 miles
(8 km)

IS THE DISTANCE FROM WHICH A FALCON CAN PERCEIVE A PIGEON.

Feet

Most birds of prey catch and kill their prey with their talons and tear away the meat with their bills. For this reason, birds' feet constitute one of the morphological characteristics of a species. The toes end in strong, sharp nails that the bird uses as pincers to catch its prey in flight. The osprey also has thorns on the soles of its feet, which help it to catch fish.

GRIFFON VULTURE
Its long toes do not have a good grasp.

FISHING EAGLE
Its toes have rough scales that look like thorns, which help it to catch fish.

GOSHAWK
It has calluses at the tips of its toes.

SPARROW HAWK
Its feet have tarsi and short, strong toes.

Talkative and Colorful

Parrots form a very attractive bird group with a great capacity for learning. This group comprises cockatoos, macaws, and parakeets. They share physical characteristics, such as a big head, a short neck, a strong hook-shaped bill, and climbing feet. They have plumage in many colors. Toucans and woodpeckers share with parrots the colors of their feathers and their type of feet. Toucans have a wider, thicker bill, but it is light. Woodpeckers are climbing birds with a strong, straight bill, a tail of stiff feathers, and a distinctive crest. They form numerous groups, and most nest in trees.

Eating, Climbing, and Chattering

Parrots use their bills to feed and to move about tree branches; they use their bills as an extension of their feet to give them support when they climb. Parrots also have a curved profile, a pointed tip on their upper mandible, and sharp edges on their lower one. These adaptations are practical when it comes to cutting and breaking fruits and seeds. The largest species like fruits with shells, such as walnuts, hazelnuts, and peanuts. The smaller ones prefer nectar and pollen, which they obtain with the help of brush-shaped bristles on their tongues. Their ability to imitate the human voice has made them very popular. However, they are far from being able to produce language. In reality, they are merely good imitators: they use their excellent memory to imitate sounds. They do this when they are hungry or when they detect the presence of unknown people.

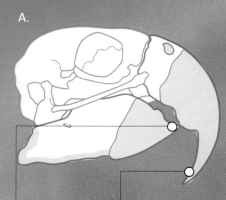

A.

UPPER PART OF THE BILL
It is where the most pressure is exerted and fruits are torn open.

HOOK
Sharp projection used to open seeds

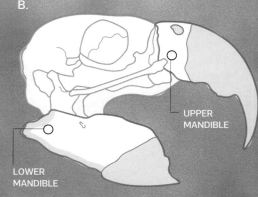

B.

UPPER MANDIBLE

LOWER MANDIBLE

UPPER AND LOWER MANDIBLES
The hook-shaped bill is flexible; the mandibles are joined to the skull by hinges. At its base, the upper mandible has a fleshy protuberance called a cere.

WOODPECKERS
hollow out tree trunks with pecks in order to build a nest and to feed on insects that eat wood.

THE HABITAT OF WOODPECKERS
They live in the woods and can often be heard there. Their adaptations to arboreal life are demonstrated by their strong, thick bills and their stiff tails, which they use for support, together with their feet. They use their hearing to locate tree-boring insects; they then peck the wood incessantly until they find them.

TOUCANS
Their big bills have serrated edges that suit their diet of fruit. They live in the South American jungles.

QUETZALS
They belong to the family Trogonidae. They have feet adapted to arboreal life. Males have brilliant plumage and long, attractive tails.

COMPARISON

American parrots vary in size, from the monk parakeet (*Myopsitta monachus*), which is 12 inches (30 cm) tall, to the hyacinth macaw (*Anodorhynchus hyacinthinus*) from South America, which is 33 inches (m) tall.

0 in or cm

MONK PARAKEET
Argentina
12–14 in (30–35 cm)

20 in (50 cm)

COCKATOO
Mexico
16–20 in
(40–50 cm)

HYACINTH MACAW
Brazil/Bolivia
39 in (100 cm)

39 in (100 cm)

The Feet

are referred to as zygodactyl. This means that two toes project forward and two project backward. Parrots appear to strut because their feet have a tibiotarsus that is shorter than that of other birds.

FEET LIKE HANDS
In some species, the left foot is longer. They use it to grab fruits and tear them with their bills.

FEATHERS AND COLORS
They have tough and lustrous plumage. An abundance of green feathers helps them to hide among the leaves. In South America, the array of colors includes hues of blue, yellow, and red.

WINGS
Usually they are short and rounded, suitable for flying among branches.

NOSTRILS
They are located at the base of the bill's upper portion.

HOOKED BILL

The Perchers Club

Passerines—or Passeriformes, the scientific name—form the widest and most diverse order of birds. What distinguishes them? Their feet are suited for perching and, therefore, for living among trees, although they can also stroll on the ground and through the brush. They inhabit terrestrial environments all over the world, from deserts to groves. Their complex sounds and songs originate from a very well-developed syrinx. Their chicks are nidicolous—that is, naked and blind at birth. In their youth, they are agile and vivacious, with very attractive, abundant, and colorful plumage.

THE SMALLEST

Passerines are small in comparison with other birds. Their size varies from 2 inches (5 cm) (bee hummingbirds, *Mellisuga helenae*) to 7 inches (19 cm) (*Chilean swallow, Tachycineta leucopyga*) to 26 inches (65 cm) (common raven, *Corvus corax*).

HUMMINGBIRDS 2 in (5 cm)
They get so much energy from nectar that they can double their body weight by eating. However, they use this energy up during their frantic flights.

SWALLOWS 7 in (19 cm)
Swallows have great agility and skill. These popular migratory birds have bodies suited for long trips.

RAVENS 26 in (65 cm)
They eat everything: fruits, insects, reptiles, small mammals, and birds. They are skillful robbers of all kinds of food.

PASSERIFORMES BIRDS

Passerines have been classified into 79 families, with more than 5,400 different species.

50%
THE PERCENTAGE OF BIRDS THAT ARE INCLUDED IN THE ORDER PASSERIFORMES

LYREBIRDS

There are only two species of these Passeriformes, and they are found only in Australia. They are very melodic and are excellent imitators of other birds. They can even imitate the sound of inanimate objects, such as horses' hooves.

Family Album

Four basic groups have been established to facilitate the study of families: passerines with wide bills; ovenbirds, whose plumage is dull and brown (ovenbirds are noted for the great care they take in building nests); lyrebirds, whose tails have two external feathers that are longer than the others; and songbirds, with their elaborate and pleasant singing. Songbirds form the most numerous and varied group; it includes swallows, goldfinches, canaries, vireos, and ravens.

SINGER

This blue-and-white swallow (*Notiochelidon cyanoleuca*) intones its pleasant and trilling chant while it flies or when it alights. Larks, goldfinches, canaries, and other passerines delight us with their trills and sounds.

HARD, SHORT BILL

The bill of a swallow is very short and tough. The swallow can use it to catch insects in flight.

SYRINX

This sound-producing organ is located at the end of the trachea. The muscles in the syrinx move the bronchial walls, which, as the air passes through, produce the melodic sounds that characterize songbirds.

Syringeal Cartilage

Tracheal Ring

Bronchial Muscles

Bronchial Ring

LIVING AT THE EXTREMES

They range from one hemisphere to the other. They raise their chicks in the north and fly to the south to spend winter there. They fly all the way to Tierra del Fuego. Their sense of direction is remarkable. They can find and reuse their nests after returning from a migration.

A In the summer, during the reproductive season, they live in the Northern Hemisphere on the North American continent. In general, neotropical migratory birds are those that reproduce above the Tropic of Cancer.

B When winter arrives in the Northern Hemisphere, they perform a mass migration to the south, occupying the Caribbean and South America. The barn swallow travels 14,000 miles (22,000 km) during its migratory trip from the United States to southern Argentina.

PERCHING FOOT

Three toes project forward, and the well-developed hallux projects backward. This type of foot allows the bird to hold on tightly to branches.

BARN SWALLOW
(*Hirundo rustica*) Barn swallows spend most of their time traveling to temperate zones.

WIDE BILLS

They are native to Africa and Asia and inhabit tropical zones with dense vegetation. They eat insects and fruits. They produce nonvocal sounds with the flapping of their wings. They do this during courtship, and the sound can be heard 200 feet (60 m) away.

OVENBIRDS AND THEIR RELATIVES

Their nests are completely covered structures, similar to ovens. Other members of this family build nests with leaves and straw, weaving interesting baskets. Still others dig tunnels in the ground.

Humans and Birds

Human beings have long taken an interest in studying these high-flying creatures. They have served as a source of food and have sometimes been used as indicators of the arrival of rain, storms, or the presence of common enemies, such as dangerous reptiles. Evidence of ancient peoples' veneration of birds can be found in documents,

ROBIN CHICKS (*Erithacus rubecula*) Although their natural habitats are humid groves, they usually seek shelter in cities, always close to water.

paintings, and reliefs. The Egyptians were the first to domesticate pigeons. Today, several species brighten up homes with their colors and cooing. Other types of birds, such as sparrows and swallows, live with us in cities. The destruction of bird habitats, through the excessive exploitation of natural resources, is one of the main causes of bird extinctions. ●

Birds and Human Culture

Birds fly, sing, dance, and have showy plumage. Because of these qualities, they have fascinated human beings throughout history. Some species, such as eagles, have played an important role in world literature because of their aggressiveness and beauty. Some birds have also been assigned symbolic meanings: doves, which currently represent peace, are one example. Human beings have also been able to make use of birds. In the past, they were often used by sailors to find land, and in other cases they were trained to hunt.

Rites and Beliefs

Birds have long enjoyed a prominent place in religion—first as totems and then as iconic representations of gods. Many religions have featured deities with the wings or heads of birds. Birds were also celestial messengers, and the future was interpreted through their flights. The crow was Apollo's messenger in ancient Greece; the Maya and Aztecs had Quetzalcóatl, their supreme god, who was named after the quetzal (a brightly colored Central American bird); and the Egyptians represented their fundamental god Horus with a falcon.

HORUS, THE FALCON, is an important god in Egyptian mythology. His eyes represent the sun and the moon, and together with Seth he watches over the boat of Ra, which carries the dead away on the Nile.

FENGHUANG was the messenger bird of Xi Wangmu, goddess of fertility and eternity in ancient China. A detail of a painting in the caves of Mogao, Dunhuang, China, is pictured above.

QUETZAL Pictured above is a detail of a Mayan ceramic piece featuring quetzals. Mesoamerican birds with long green tails, from which, according to myth, the god Quetzalcóatl took his clothing and name: "feathered serpent."

GARUDA FRESCO Pictured above is a winged deity, featured on a fragment of a mural from the Hindu temple of Garuda, in Ananta Samarkhom, Bangkok, Thailand.

Falconry

This practice originated in Asia, in the homeland of the nomadic Mongols—descendants of the Genghis Khan—where, to this day, it is commonly used as a form of subsistence by part of the population. It consists of using birds of prey (mainly falcons) to hunt. Trained birds are typically carried, hooded, and perched on their masters' arms. When released, they fly at high altitudes looking for prey, and then dive toward the ground to hunt it. They carry the prey back to their masters, who reward them with food. The basic training process takes a little over a month and a half.

ELEMENTS

Birds and masters wear specific clothes. In addition to gloves, hoods, and straps, radio transmitters are now also used to locate the birds as they fly.

HOOD

FALCON

TRANSMITTER

GUANTE

LASH

GLOVE   STRAPS

PIGEON Sometimes their numbers in urban areas become excessive.

SPARROW The sparrow is one of the birds best adapted to the urban environment.

NORTH AMERICAN INDIGENOUS MAN wearing a war costume covered with feathers

COMPETITOR BIRDS

When birds share a habitat with humans, they often compete for resources (light, water, space, and nutrients). This is the case with birds that feed on cultivated crops. Urban areas, which have buildings that offer good nesting sites, attract many birds. This fact can be commonly observed in squares and open spaces, where pigeons and sparrows form veritable flocks.

Bird Symbolism

Throughout history and across cultures, human beings have used birds to symbolize several concepts. The fascination that their flight creates was a source of inspiration for such interpretations. Today the strongest and most widespread association is that of the flight of birds with freedom. In distant times (and in not so distant times), however, birds have represented many other things, from fertility and happiness, with their spring songs, to deep mourning, in the case of crows and vultures. Wisdom has been associated with owls, and shrewdness with crows. According to a certain modern tale, storks are responsible for bringing babies, and eggs are the universal symbol of gestation.

EAGLE

In Greek mythology, it was the symbol of Zeus. The Romans used it on their legions' banners. For many native North American cultures, it represented war, and it was the emblem of feudal lords and emperors. Today, it is the national symbol of Mexico and the United States.

DOVE

Doves currently stand for peace, but in ancient Greece, Syria, and Phoenicia, they were used as oracles. In Mesopotamia and Babylon, they embodied fertility. For Christians, they symbolize the Holy Spirit and the Virgin Mary.

Dressing Up in Feathers

Almost all cultures have used bird feathers for decorative and ritualistic purposes. Their use as ornaments extended to North and South America, Africa, and the Western Pacific. North American indigenous peoples featured them on their war outfits. Hawaiian kings wore them on their royal costumes, and the Mayans and Aztecs used them in works of art.

How to Get to Know Birds

Ornithology (from the Greek *ornitho*, "bird," and *logos*, "science") is a branch of zoology that studies birds. Ornithologists and a great number of bird lovers, who enthusiastically want to know more about these creatures, carry out the task methodically and patiently. They observe, analyze, and register birds' sounds, colors, movements, and behavior in their natural environments. To undertake this fieldwork, they develop methods and techniques and use technological resources to track specimens and learn about what happens to them during given times of the year.

STUDIES

Many studies on anatomy, physiology, and genetics of different bird species are carried out in laboratories.

WORK CLOTHES

Although seemingly a small detail, clothes can be a hindrance. They should be comfortable and soft, appropriate for the weather, and of colors that blend into the environment.

BINOCULARS

They make it possible to see details in color and shape without disturbing the birds. Their usefulness depends on the power of their lenses.

CAMERA WITH ZOOM LENS

A camera with a powerful lens provides the opportunity to record details that simple cameras cannot.

TAPE RECORDER

Recording birds' noises and songs makes it possible to distinguish among birds. Experts can identify species by listening to their recordings.

Direct Observation

Observing in a bird's natural habitat provides much information. For the greatest success, bird-watchers typically place themselves in front of rocks or trees in order not to form a silhouette. An alternative technique is to create a hiding place, such as a hollow cardboard rock. In both cases, the watcher needs to be facing away from the sun and must be prepared to stay for a long time.

Catching Birds

MIST NET
These fine nets are usually placed over swamps or marshes, and they can catch small birds. Once the birds are identified with a ring or some other tag, they are set free.

CANNON NETS
These nets are "shot" over birds using cannons or rockets. They unroll and catch birds as they are eating or resting. They are used to catch large birds.

HELIGOLAND TRAP
It consists of a large barbed-wire funnel or corridor that ends in a box. Birds caught like this are tagged so that they can be monitored and studied later on.

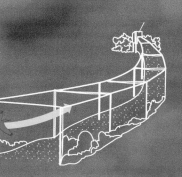

Scientists take advantage of molting to study penguins. When they are changing plumage, these birds stand on their legs, which makes it difficult to place or observe any rings on their legs. Instead, strips are placed around their wings, or electronic chips are implanted in their skin. The latter technique is less harmful because it does not potentially hinder the animal.

The Marking of Captured Birds

➤ This technique provides data on migration, survival, and reproduction rates, among other data. The bird should not suffer adverse effects in its behavior, longevity, or social interactions. Under no circumstances should this procedure hurt a bird. To avoid hurting birds, rings are designed to be placed on them rapidly and easily, yet to stay in place until the research is completed.

RINGED
Numbered aluminum rings are used. When placing one on a bird, one should make sure that it slides and turns around the tibiotarsus to avoid hurting the bird or causing it to change its activity.

WING MARKERS
They are very visible and can be codified for individual identification. They stay on the bird for long periods of time and are normally used on birds of prey.

NECK MARKERS
When placed appropriately, necklaces are effective markers with few adverse effects on geese, swans, or other aquatic birds with long necks.

NASAL MARKERS
These are colored, numbered plastic disks placed on the bill. They are fastened to the nasal orifices of aquatic birds.

PAINTS AND DYES
Birds that visit environments with dense vegetation are normally marked with nontoxic colorings on the feathers of their highest and most visible body parts.

Among Us

The urban environment presents opportunities for birds. It offers advantages in finding food and shelter. People, young and old, give bread crumbs to these interested visitors. When birds come to cities, houses and parks offer them protection. They can find more options when it comes to building a nest. Seagulls and owls have changed their behavior by adapting to the city, and other species, such as some sparrows, are no longer able to survive without a human presence. However, not everything is an advantage. In the city, birds have to face dangers and obstacles that do not exist in their natural habitat: a utility wire or a car can be fatal. ●

Where to Find Them

In big cities, groups of birds can be found in different areas. Busy and noisy areas, such as squares, parks, and gardens, attract many species. Calm, deserted spaces, such as cemeteries or deserted buildings, are chosen by birds in search of peace. Other places where birds choose to eat and sleep include plots and landfills with lots of food, as well as nooks in high places, such as balconies, belfries, and roosts.

URBAN CENTERS
With the arrival of cold weather, different bird species from the countryside and the mountains come to the city. In general, they stay until the beginning of spring. In the winter, more birds, such as chiffchaffs, great tits, and robins, can be observed in cities.

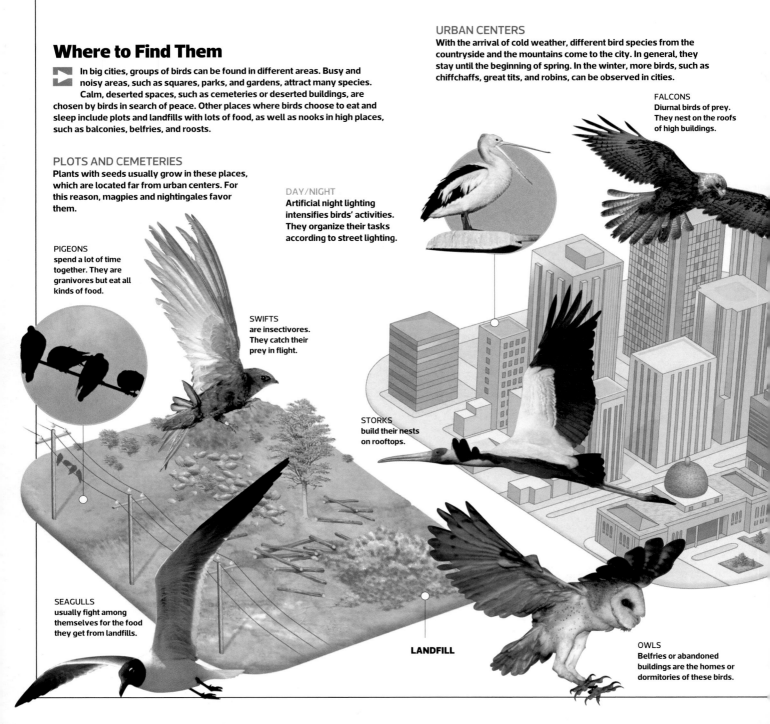

FALCONS
Diurnal birds of prey. They nest on the roofs of high buildings.

PLOTS AND CEMETERIES
Plants with seeds usually grow in these places, which are located far from urban centers. For this reason, magpies and nightingales favor them.

DAY/NIGHT
Artificial night lighting intensifies birds' activities. They organize their tasks according to street lighting.

PIGEONS
spend a lot of time together. They are granivores but eat all kinds of food.

SWIFTS
are insectivores. They catch their prey in flight.

STORKS
build their nests on rooftops.

SEAGULLS
usually fight among themselves for the food they get from landfills.

LANDFILL

OWLS
Belfries or abandoned buildings are the homes or dormitories of these birds.

PARKS AND GARDENS

Royal peacocks and green peafowls share these places, where they can find the microhabitats of insects on which they feed. Parks and gardens may have ponds that are visited by other bird species as well. Few species nest in these places because these spaces offer little quiet.

BLACKBIRDS
were originally migratory, but as they adjusted to cities, they became nonmigratory.

SPARROWS
Small birds with a highly varied diet

The Urban Environment

This setting is characterized by environmental and climatic factors that are different from the natural ones. It has more varieties of plants, higher average temperatures, less wind, more rain, cloudier skies, and less solar radiation. Polluted air and soil are harmful factors for both humans and birds.

10%
RAIN
INCREASE

15%
WIND
INTENSITY DECREASE

1.5°
TEMPERATURE
INCREASE DOWNTOWN

GROVE

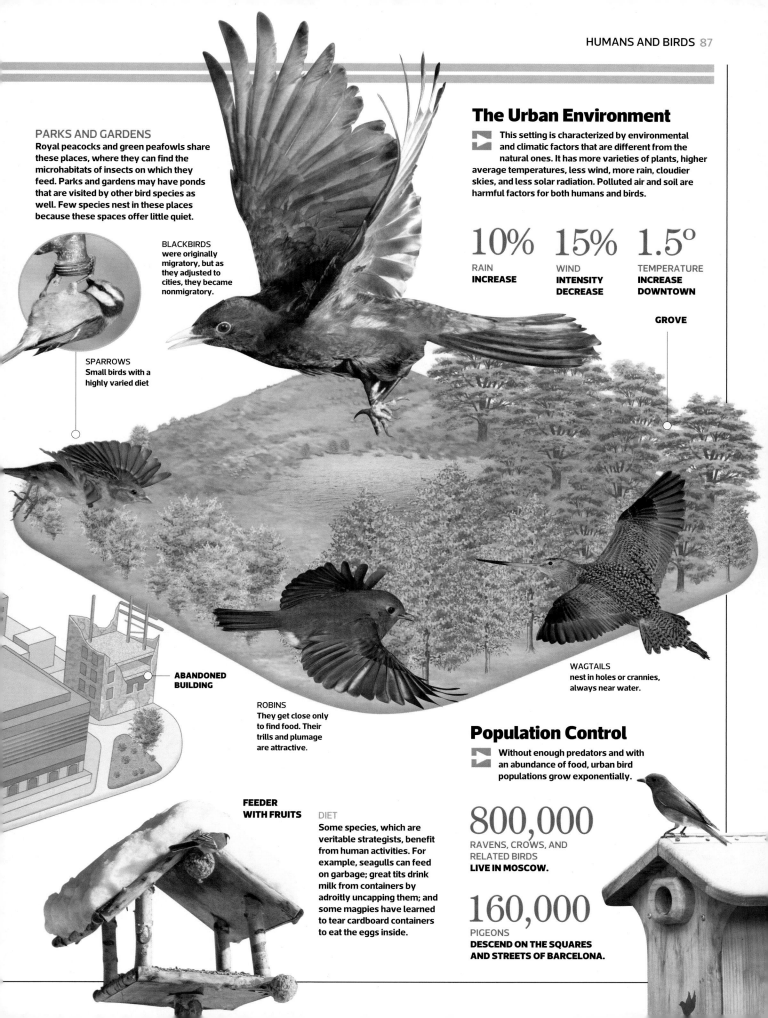

ABANDONED BUILDING

ROBINS
They get close only to find food. Their trills and plumage are attractive.

WAGTAILS
nest in holes or crannies, always near water.

Population Control

Without enough predators and with an abundance of food, urban bird populations grow exponentially.

800,000
RAVENS, CROWS, AND RELATED BIRDS
LIVE IN MOSCOW.

160,000
PIGEONS
DESCEND ON THE SQUARES AND STREETS OF BARCELONA.

FEEDER WITH FRUITS

DIET
Some species, which are veritable strategists, benefit from human activities. For example, seagulls can feed on garbage; great tits drink milk from containers by adroitly uncapping them; and some magpies have learned to tear cardboard containers to eat the eggs inside.

Bird Domesticators

The breeding of birds in captivity has great social and economic value. This activity is carried out all over the world on industrial poultry farms and family farms where birds are raised for consumption and sale. A great variety of domestic birds have been developed from species inhabiting natural environments. We use their flesh and eggs as food and their feathers in coats to protect us against the cold. We also use birds for communication and as colorful and melodic pets. They are so dependent on people that in some cases they cannot survive when they are freed. ●

CAGED
Canaries, native to the Canary Islands, have been selectively bred by humans for nearly four centuries.

At Your Service

▶ Domestic birds have been bred from the following orders: Galliformes (hens, quails, turkeys, and pheasants), Anseriformes (ducks and geese), Columbiformes (pigeons), Passeriformes (canaries), and Psittaciformes (parakeets and parrots). In poultry farming, they are divided according to their use: barnyard birds (Galliformes, Anseriformes, and Columbiformes) and companion birds or pets (Passeriformes and Psittaciformes). Commercial poultry farming of barnyard birds generates high revenues worldwide. Farmers can take advantage of the fact that birds are very active during the day, that they readily live in groups, and that they have a high reproductive rate due to polygamous behavior. Pets have commercial appeal, with their colorful plumage, ability to express themselves, and friendliness toward humans. These characteristics make them much-appreciated pets.

TURKEY
On the American continent, these birds were domesticated by the indigenous pre-Columbians from a wild Mexican species called *Meleagris gallopavo gallopavo*.

GOOSE
Contemporary domestic breeds descend from wild Asian and eastern European species. They are voracious, which makes fattening them easy.

DUCK
These birds are an important source of food in Southeast Asia. In Central and South America, the consumption of ducks is less widespread.

AIRMAIL
For more than 1,700 years, human beings have used pigeons to send messages. Armies have used them as communication aids during wars. Pigeon keeping is the practice of breeding and preparing pigeons to become messengers, a task that makes the most of their agility and intelligence.

BIRD FLU

This disease, also called avian influenza A, is caused by a virus whose strains have various levels of virulence. It disseminated from Asian markets, where the overcrowding of domestic birds is common. This promoted the spread of the disease to wild birds. As of 2006, more than 30 million birds had succumbed to this disease. Cats, pigs, and human beings have also been infected.

50%
THE COMMOTION AND FEAR OVER DISEASE HAVE REDUCED THE DEMAND FOR THE CONSUMPTION OF DOMESTIC BIRDS IN MAJOR EUROPEAN CITIES BY HALF.

PATHS INTO THE BODY
Digestive Tract
Urogenital Tract

Conjunctiva
Respiratory Tract
Needles
Skin
Wounds

SIZE COMPARISON
Bacteria ———
Virus ———

2 The virus can be transmitted to the most common of domestic birds: chickens.

3 The H5N1 virus is transmitted to humans through direct contact with domestic birds.

1 Ducks carry the H5N1 virus but are immune to this disease.

Farm Model

When compared to other farm animals, birds grow and reproduce easily. They need to have a place with appropriate temperature, humidity, and ventilation in order to yield the desired amount of meat or eggs. For this reason, it is necessary to maintain continuous environmental and sanitary control of the area in which they are bred. Ideally they should be able to walk, run, scratch the earth in search of food, and take sunbaths. Additionally, to protect them from predators and from inclement weather, it is important to shelter them in coops. This allows them to rest peacefully and sleep at night.

QUENCHING THIRST
Ten chickens drink from 0.5 to 0.8 gallon (2–3 l) of water a day. The farmer provides them with water in troughs, which are placed all over the henhouse.

MIXED DIET
Birds look for insects and plant shoots as they peck the soil. The breeder complements this diet with nutritionally balanced foods.

DOMESTICATION IN HISTORY

The domestication of birds is a very old activity, as shown by records from different cultures in different parts of the world. It was related to the adoption of a sedentary way of life by human populations.

5000 BC	2000 BC	1492
India There are records of domestic geese in India, beginning in 5000 BC.	**Far East** Descendants of the royal duck (*Anas platyrhynchos*) were domesticated in this area of the Asian continent (what is now China).	**Mexico** The Spanish colonizers encountered turkeys domesticated by inhabitants of the New World.

Endangered Species

S ince early civilization, people have affected the Earth's environment. The cutting of trees in rainforests and woodlands has destroyed many bird habitats, the loss of which is the leading cause of bird extinctions today. Also, the introduction of animals such as cats, dogs, and rats to new areas has created a threat for many bird species. Indirect poisoning with pesticides, the trafficking of exotic birds as pets, and the sale of feathers have done further damage to many species. Fortunately, all is not lost. The first step to conserving the world's avifauna is to learn about the extinction of birds and its magnitude. ●

The Most Important Causes

Birds are very sensitive to changes in their habitats, and this is the main cause of extinction (87 percent of species are affected by it). Excessive hunting is another of the greatest dangers, affecting 29 percent of the endangered species in the world. The introduction of foreign species is yet another major danger, jeopardizing 28 percent of species. In addition, the intervention of human beings through the destruction of habitats and the introduction of pollution combined with the occurrence of natural disasters harms more than 10 percent of species.

POISONING

Most birds of prey are endangered by the excessive use of nonbiodegradable pesticides.

Pesticides

Granivorous Birds

Birds of Prey

PEREGRINE FALCON

1
Pesticides are sprayed on crops to eliminate pests, and they stick to the seeds.

2
Small quantities of poison in seeds accumulate in larger amounts in birds and other granivorous animals.

3
Birds of prey eat the granivores. The increasing use of pesticides impacts hunting birds the most.

CALIFORNIA CONDOR
Gymnogyps californianus
Until 1978, there were 30 specimens in the wild. Bred in captivity, new specimens have been set free since 1993. Their adaptation is being studied.

● Wood Buffalo

Atlantic Ocean

NORTH AMERICA

UNITED STATES

○ California

Everglades ●

CENTRAL AMERICA

Pacific Ocean

HYACINTH MACAW
Anodorhynchus hyacinthinus
It is estimated that 1,000 to 9,000 specimens live in the Amazon.

COLOMBIA

ECUADOR ○

Amazon ○

BRAZIL

PERU ○

ROYAL CINCLODES
Cinclodes aricomae
live on humid mountain ranges, at altitudes between 11,500 and 15,000 feet (3,500–4,500 m). Their number is unknown.

MANGROVE FINCH
Camarhynchus heliobates
There are about 100 remaining species on the Galapagos Islands.

SOUTH AMERICA

● Nahuel Huapí

SAVING THE PEREGRINE FALCON FROM EXTINCTION

1942
There were 350 couples of peregrine falcons in the United States.

1960
Peregrine falcons disappeared in the wild because of excessive use of pesticides (DDT and dieldrin).

1970
Falcons were bred in captivity at Cornell University, to be set free later.

1986
850 birds were set free in the southern United States.

BirdLife
INTERNATIONAL

BirdLife International
It monitors endangered species and develops conservation programs.

CLASSIFICATION OF RISK

Extinct in the Wild
Species surviving
only in captivity

Critical Risk
Extinction is
imminent

Endangered
Fast-decreasing
population

Vulnerable
High risk of
extinction in the wild

BIRDS OF THE WORLD

According to BirdLife International 2000 there are 9,856 registered species, of which 1,226 are threatened by extinction.

88%
Non-
threatened
species

12%
Threatened
species

Threatened species

669 Vulnerable
363 Endangered
190 In critical danger
4 Extinct

EXTINCT BIRDS

Although the responsibility of human beings is undeniable, many species became extinct because of natural phenomena. However, all the extinctions from the 18th century to date are related to human activities.

129 SPECIES HAVE GONE EXTINCT SINCE THE 18TH CENTURY.

Dodo from Mauritius
Quickly exterminated by colonizers and seafarers in the 17th century

INDIAN VULTURE
Gyps indicus
Its population has decreased significantly as a result of the veterinary use of diclofenac. The vulture eats the carrion of animals treated with this drug and becomes poisoned.

EUROPE

ASIA

AFRICA

Pacific Ocean

BENGAL VULTURE
Gyps bengalensis
From 1996 to date, its population has fallen by 95 percent, especially in India.

CHINA

○ INDIA

PHILIPPINES

PHILIPPINE COCKATOO
Cacatua haematuropygia
It is estimated that there are between 1,000 and 4,000 individuals remaining. It was hunted indiscriminately.

Indian Ocean

● **Prince Albert**

Tsavo ●

Serengeti ●

LEGEND

● SHELTERS AND SANCTUARIES FOR ENDANGERED BIRDS

INDONESIA

Celebes ○

YELLOW-CRESTED COCKATOO
Cacatua sulphurea
In three generations, its population fell by 80 percent because of hunting.

Wankie ●

CAMPBELL ISLAND TEAL
Anas nesiotis
Only 50 individuals remain because of the introduction of mammals to the island.

20%
OF THE EARTH'S SURFACE IS HOME TO ALL ENDANGERED BIRD SPECIES.

OCEANIA

● **Krüger**

Alarming Data

Five percent of the planet's surface houses three fourths of endangered species. This area coincides with tropical regions where biodiversity is greater. For this reason, tropical countries top the list to the right. On some islands, the proportion of endangered birds is very high: in the Philippines and in New Zealand, it includes 35 to 42 percent of avian fauna.

NEW ZEALAND

Country	Value
Indonesia	118
Brazil	115
Colombia	78
China	76
Peru	75
India	74
Philippines	42
Ecuador	35
New Zealand	25
United States	20

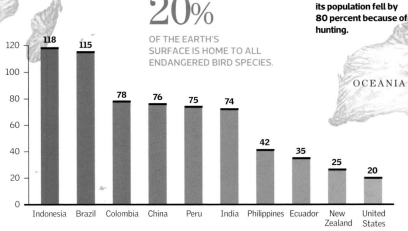

Glossary

Adaptation

Change in the body of a bird or another animal that allows it to reproduce better in a given environment.

Adaptive Radiation

Evolution of an initial species, adapted to a given way of life, into other species, each adapted to its own way of life.

Aerodynamic

Having an appropriate shape to decrease resistance to the air. Birds' bodies are aerodynamic.

Alulae

Rigid feathers whose function is to decrease air turbulence during flight.

Amino Acid

Molecule from which proteins are produced.

Ancestor

Progenitor, more or less remote, that passes down a set of characteristics to its descendants.

Angle of Attack

The change in position of a bird's wing to increase or decrease speed and altitude while hunting prey by air.

Apterylae

Naked areas of the skin where feathers do not grow.

Atrophy

Significant decrease in the size of an organ. The wings of nonflying birds have undergone atrophy during evolution.

Barbs

Thin, straight, parallel blades, perpendicular to the shaft. They resemble the leaves of a palm tree.

Bill

Hard cover of a bird's mandibles; also called the bill.

Biodiversity

Variety of species that live in a given natural or artificial environment.

Biogeographic Regions

Geographic regions that biologists analyze to determine the distribution of animals and other living organisms, according to the geographic conditions of a place. Migratory birds usually travel through different biogeographic regions between winter and summer.

Biped

Aero-terrestrial animal that walks on its posterior limbs. Birds are bipeds.

Briny

Water sample or body of water containing between 0.08 and 4.25 ounces (0.5-30 g) of salt per gallon of aqueous solution.

Bronchus

Each of the branches into which the trachea divides. The syrinx originates in the bronchi.

Calamus

The lower part of the vane that is wider, hollow, and, in general, naked. The feather is attached to the skin through the calamus.

Camouflage

A characteristic that enables the animal to blend into its environment. It allows the animal to go unnoticed in the presence of predators.

Carnivore

An animal that feeds on meat.

Carrion

The remains of dead animals used as food by some birds or other animals. Vultures are scavengers (i.e., animals that feed on carrion).

Center of Gravity

Point at which the sum of all the gravitational forces that act on a body converge.

Cere

Thin skin layer that covers the base of the bill.

Chick

A baby bird that has just come out of the eggshell and that has not yet left the nest. Its diet and safety depend on its parents.

Chorion

One of the coverings that wraps the embryo of reptiles, birds, and mammals.

Class

One of the many divisions scientists use to classify animals. Birds form a class of their own.

Climate

Average temperature, humidity, and pressure that determine the atmospheric conditions of a region and that are related to other geographic characteristics of that region.

Cloaca

The widened and dilatable final portion of the intestine of a bird or other animal in which the urinogenital tubes converge.

Courtship

Behavior patterns that males and females follow to try to attract partners.

Coverts

Layers of contour feathers that provide a bird's body and wings with support and an aerodynamic surface.

Crepuscular

Active at dawn or twilight, when there is little light.

Crest

Extended or raised feathers located on the upper part of a bird's head.

Crop

Membranous sac that communicates with a bird's esophagus, where food is softened.

Dermal Papilla

Structure from which a feather develops. It is composed of epidermal and dermal cells.

Display

Behavior directed at attracting the attention of a partner. It can also be done to threaten or distract another animal.

Distribution

Place where a species is located. It includes the area the species occupies in different seasons.

Down Feather

A very thin and light feather, similar to silk, that birds have underneath their external plumage. Down feathers constitute the first plumage of chicks.

Ecosystem

Community of living beings whose vital processes are interrelated and develop according to the physical factors of the same environment.

Egg

Large rounded shell, laid by a female bird, that contains a yolk and a white. If fertilized, the egg has a tiny embryo that will develop into a chick (the chick feeds itself on the yolk and white). When ready, the chick will break the eggshell.

Egg Tooth

Sharp calcium growth, in the shape of a tooth, that forms on the tip of a chick's bill during the embryonic phase. The chick uses the egg tooth to break its shell at birth.

Environment

The natural conditions, such as vegetation and land, that surround animals and influence their development and behavior.

Epiphysis

Endocrine gland located below the corpus callosum in the brain. It produces a hormone that regulates sexual activity.

Evolution

Gradual process of change that a species undergoes to adjust to the environment.

Extinct

No longer existing. Many bird species are now extinct (for example, ictiornites).

Feather

Each unit of the covering (plumage) of a bird. The feathers are composed of a hard substance called keratin. They have a long quill, to which two blades are joined. The blades—formed by a great number of barbs, uniformly distributed—give the feather its shape and color.

Fertilization

Union of the reproductive cells of a male and a female that will create a new individual.

Field Mark

Natural distinct feature or artificial identification of an individual of a bird species that helps ornithologists distinguish it from other individuals of the same or other avian species.

Fledgling

Very young bird that lives in the nest where it was raised.

Fossils

Vestiges of ancient creatures of different types (vegetal or animal) on a stone substratum. Fossils can be found in the geologic strata of the Earth's surface.

Gastric Juice

Set of fluids produced by the stomach glands of birds and other animals.

Gizzard

Muscular stomach of a bird. It is very robust, especially in granivores, and it is used to grind and soften the food by means of mechanical pressure. The food arrives at the gizzard mixed with digestive juices.

Gland

Type of structure that is present in most multicellular living beings. It produces substances that act either inside or outside a bird's body.

Gonad

Organ that makes male or female gametes. In birds, the testicles and ovaries are gonads.

Granivore

Bird that feeds on seeds or grains. Many birds are granivores (for example, parrots and toucans).

Gular Sac

Skin fragment in the shape of a sac that hangs from the lower mandible of certain birds (for example, pelicans).

Habitat

Native or natural environment of an animal or plant.

Hatching

Cracking of the eggshell so that the bird cancome out .

Histologic

Related to tissues and their study. When the anatomy of a bird is studied, the tissues that form the bird's organs are analyzed.

Hormones

Secretion of certain glands that circulates through the body. They excite, inhibit, or regulate the activities of organs or of systems of organs.

Horn

Made of horn or of a consistency similar to that of horn. The bill of birds is hornlike.

Hypophysis

Internal secretion organ located at the hollow of the skull's base (called silla turca). It is composed of two lobes: one anterior and glandular and the other posterior and nervous. The hormones produced by the hypophysis influence growth and sexual development, among other things.

Hypothalamus

Region of the encephalon located at the cerebral base, joined to the hypophysis by a nerve stem, in which important centers for vegetative life are found.

Incubation

The act of keeping the eggs warm so that the embryos inside can grow and hatch. Usually the chick's parents use their own bodies to warm the eggs, but some birds use sand or decomposing plants to cover them.

Insectivore

Bird that eats insects as part of its diet.

Instinct

Innate behavior that a bird or other animal develops and that is not learned. The offspring of ducks start to swim by instinct.

Invertebrate

Animal that lacks a spinal column. Worms, crabs, and jellyfish are examples.

Lethargy

Sleep through which a bird can reduce its cardiac rhythm and its body temperature to save energy, especially at night and during extended periods of cold.

Malpighian Layer

Layer of epithelial cells that forms the bird's epidermis.

Mangrove Swamp

Type of ecosystem often considered a type of biome. It is composed of trees that are very tolerant to salt. These trees are found in the intertidal zone of tropical coasts. Areas with mangrove swamps include estuaries and coastal zones.

Migration

The movement of birds from one region to another; it usually takes place in the spring and fall. It is also common among other species of animals.

Molt

Process through which birds lose old worn feathers, replacing them with new ones.

Monogamous

Birds that mate with only one individual of the opposite sex. Many penguins have monogamous behavior.

Morphology

Study of the form of an object or structure. For instance, the morphology of the feet of birds is an area of study.

Nectar

Sweet and sugary secretions found in flowers that attract birds and other animals. Hummingbirds feed on nectar.

Nidicolous

A helpless chick that depends on its parents' care after birth.

Nidifugous

A chick that can move and leave the nest as soon as it breaks its shell. In less than a day, such chicks can move agilely.

Nocturnal

Active at night. Many birds of prey, such as owls, specialize in nocturnal hunting.

Nutrient

Any substance obtained through diet that participates in the vital functions of a living being.

Omnivore

Bird that has a varied diet, including animal and vegetal foods.

Pelagic

Birds that live in areas over open waters, away from the coast.

Pellet (Bolus)

Small, hard mass that some birds regurgitate (vomit). It contains parts of the food that they could not digest, such as bones, fur, feathers, and teeth.

Pigment

Substance that colors the skin, feathers, or tissues of animals and plants.

Piscivore

Birds living in continental or oceanic waters that feed on fish.

Pollution

A consequence of human actions for natural environments. The emission of industrial gases into the atmosphere, for example, produces pollution.

Polygamy

Reproductive relationship between one animal of one sex and several animals of the other. When one male mates with several females, it is called polygyny. Only rarely do females have multiple male reproductive partners (polyandry).

Population

Set of individuals of the same species that live together in the same space at the same time

Predator

Animal that hunts other animals. Birds of prey hunt other birds, mammals, and vertebrates.

Prey

Animal hunted by another to serve as food for the latter. Animals that hunt prey are called predators.

Protein

Organic macromolecule that is part of living beings. By including proteins in their diet, birds get the necessary amino acids to build their own organs.

Protein Cord

Embryonic structure: each of the two filaments that sustain the yolk of the egg within the white.

Proventriculus

The first portion of the stomach, or the true stomach, of a bird. The other portion of a bird's stomach is the gizzard.

Rectrices

Technical term used by ornithologists to describe a bird's tail feathers.

Scale

Dermic or epidermic layer that totally or partially covers the feet of birds. They are reptilian vestiges.

Song

Sound or series of sounds produced by a bird to demarcate its territory or to find a mate. The songs of birds can be simple or elaborate, and some are very melodic.

Songbirds

Singing birds. Passerines include songbirds.

Species

Set of individuals that recognize themselves as belonging to the same reproductive unit.

Sternum

Central chest bone. The sternum of flying birds has a large surface in which muscles are inserted.

Survival

A bird's ability to face the demands of its environment and of intra- and interspecies relationships.

Swamp

Depression on the ground in which water is gathered, sometimes called a marsh. Its bottom is more or less boggy. It is the habitat of many wading birds.

Thermal

Hot air current that rises. Many birds make use of it to gain height effortlessly.

Theropods

Group to which carnivorous dinosaurs belong.

Training

Teaching an animal new skills. Carrier pigeons are trained.

Tundra

Vast plains without trees in the Arctic regions of northern Asia, Europe, and North America.

Uropygial Gland

Produces an oily secretion that birds, using their bills, spread on their feathers to make them impermeable.

Vertebrate

Animals that have a spinal column, such as birds, fish, reptiles, amphibians, and mammals.

Virus

Infectious agent that depends on a living being to reproduce. Avian flu is transmitted this way.

Vulnerable

Birds that are endangered in their natural habitats.

Yolk

Yellow part of the egg. If the egg is fertilized, a small embryo grows that will use the yolk (and white) as food.

Young

Bird or any other animal at an early stage of life. Some young show color patterns that are very different from that of adults of the same species, which makes it difficult for predators to identify them.

For More Information

American Bird Conservancy
P.O. Box 249
4249 Loudoun Ave.
The Plains, VA 20198-2237
(540) 253-5780
Website: https://abcbirds.org
Twitter: @ABCbirds1
Instagram: @americanbirdconservancy
This conservancy aims to protect birds native to America, in particular, and restore their habitats across the Americas.

National Audubon Society
225 Varick St., 7th Fl.
New York, NY 10014
(212) 979-3196
Website: http://www.audubon.org
Twitter: @audubonsociety
The National Audubon Society is a nonprofit organization that helps preserve the ecosystems birds inhabit and joins bird enthusi-
    asts from all over.

National Wildlife Federation (NWF)
11100 Wildlife Center Drive
Reston, VA 20190-5362
(800) 822-9919
Website: http://www.nwf.org
Twitter: @NWF
Instagram: @nationalwildlife
The NWF seeks to protect and restore wildlife habitats and connect the next generation of Americans to nature.

North American Bird Conservation Initiative (NABCI)
1100 First Street NE
Washington, DC 20002
(202) 838-3475
Website: http://nabci-us.org
The NABCI is a collection of governmental agencies and private organizations that work together to establish, meet, and maintain
    common bird conservation goals.

Wild Bird Fund
565 Columbus Avenue
New York, NY 10024
(646) 306-2862
Website: https://www.wildbirdfund.org
Twitter: @wildbirdfund
Instagram: @wildbirdfund
New York City's Wild Bird Fund provides medical attention and support to injured birds in an effort to release them back into the
    wild.

For Further Reading

Ackerman, Jennifer. *The Genius of Birds.* New York, NY: Penguin Books, 2016.

Barnes, Simon. *The Meaning of Birds.* New York, NY: Pegasus Books, 2018.

Brewer, David. *Birds New to Science: Fifty Years of Avian Discoveries.* London, UK: Christopher Helm, 2018.

Dunne, Pete. *Birds of Prey: Hawks, Eagles, Falcons, and Vultures of North America.* New York, NY: Houghton Mifflin Harcourt, 2016.

Emery, Nathan. *Bird Brain: An Exploration of Avian Intelligence.* Princeton, NJ: The Ivy Press, 2016.

Lederer, Roger. *Beaks, Bones, and Bird Songs: How the Struggle for Survival Has Shaped Birds and Their Behavior.* Portland, OR: Timber Press, 2016.

Robbins, Jim. *The Wonder of Birds: What They Tell Us About Ourselves, the World, and a Better Future.* New York, NY: Spiegel & Grau, 2017.

Strycker, Noah. *Birding Without Borders: An Obsession, a Quest, and the Biggest Year in the World.* New York, NY: Houghton Mifflin Harcourt, 2017.

Strycker, Noah. *The Thing with Feathers: The Surprising Lives of Birds and What They Reveal About Being Human.* New York, NY: Riverhead Books, 2014.

Index

A

adaptation
aquatic life, 5
cellulose digestion, 57
environment, 66
flightless birds, 29
flying, 8f, 12, 24–25
foot, 20–21
hatching, 53
marine birds, 70, 71
perching, 13, 79
swimming, 68
urban habitats, 83
walking, 7
adaptive radiation, 62
aero-terrestrial habitat, 65
African ostrich
flightless birds, 68–69
weight, 8
Afrotropic region, 67
albatross
birth, 52
classification, 64
gliding, 35
incubation (egg), 52
migration routes, 59
wings, 29
altitudinal migration, 58
anatomy
external features, 8–9
internal organs, 14–15
skeleton and musculature, 12–13
*See also specific body parts by name,
for example,* **wing**
ankle, 21
annual life cycle, 42–43
Anseriformes (bird classification), 64, 72
Antarctic bird: *See* **penguin**
apteria, 27
Apterygiformes (bird classification), 65, 69
aquatic bird
classification, 64, 65
foot adaptation, 20

physical adaptations, 5
powder down, 27
See also **marine bird**
arboreal theory (evolution), 24
Archaeopteryx, 10–11
arctic tern, migration, 39, 58
aricari, bill, 19
artery, 15
Asia
bird domestication, 89
migration routes, 59
Australasia, 67
Australian bowerbird, courtship behavior, 46
avian influenza A, 88
Aztec culture, 82

B

bald eagle
birds of prey, 74
talons, 21
bar-headed goose
flight altitude, 38
migration routes, 59
barn swallow, migration, 58, 59, 79
bat, wing, 24
beak: *See* **bill**
Bengal vulture, 91
bill, 18–19
birds of prey, 74
ducks, 73
food filtration, 56
identification, 9
modern bird, 12
parrot, 76
binocular vision, 17
binoculars, 84
biodiversity
endangered species, 90–91
geographical regions, 66–67
running birds, 69
biogeographic region, 66–67
bird flu: *See* **avian influenza A**

bird of prey, 74–75
pesticide poisoning, 90
vision, 17
birdcall,
communication, 44
warnings, 61
birdsong, communication, 44–45
birdwatching, 84
black grouse, courtship display, 31
black swan, flight speed, 38
blackbird, urban habitats, 87
blood circulation: *See* **circulatory system**
blue-and-white swallow, 80
blue-footed booby, courtship behavior, 43
bone: *See* **skeletal system**
brain
Archaeopteryx, 10
sound production, 44
breathing: *See* **respiratory system**
brown pelican, 70
Bubo capensis, 6, 7
Buffon, Georges-Louis Leclerc, Count de, 66

C

California condor, captive breeding, 90
call: *See* **birdcall**
camera, 84
camouflage
defense strategies, 60
molting, 32
Campbell Island teal, 91
canary, 88
cannon net, 85
Cape gannet
marine birds, 70
migration routes, 58
captive breeding, 90
carnivorous bird
gizzard, 14
See also **bird of prey**